To

_____

From

_____

Date

_____

STRONG

DEVOTIONS

to Live a Powerful
& Passionate Life

LISA BEVERE

THOMAS NELSON
Since 1798

Published in Nashville, Tennessee, by Thomas Nelson. Thomas Nelson is a registered trademark of HarperCollins Christian Publishing, Inc.

CONTENTS

PART 6 – *Strong in Battle*

PART 7 – *Strong in Grace*

Strong
in God

IT'S OKAY TO BE STRONG

God is strong, and he wants you strong.
EPHESIANS 6:10 MSG

As we begin this journey of becoming strong, let's first settle something in our hearts:

Strong is not wrong.

Too often Christian women are associated with weakness rather than strength. Sometimes religion has taught us to hide rather than to rise. It is true that we are called to be meek, but not weak. Meek is best defined as strength under control. Both Moses and Jesus were meek, but not weak. The meek know their strength comes from God. Esther was meek, but she was no weakling. The meek are also the humble because they understand that their strength comes from a higher power. The meek know how and when to fight, but they are not looking for one.

Strength is a two-edged sword that can be used as a weapon of destruction or a means of release that sets the captives free. It is not unusual that the first captive that requires release is ourselves.

This life requires strength. And as we live longer, life gets harder. Living godly in a godless culture will require much more strength than you or I can muster on our own. Thankfully we are not on our own. We are going to examine the following verses from Ephesians that outline why each of us must embrace the challenge and become strong. After describing how we interact in relationships, Paul begins Ephesians 6:10–18 with "Finally, be strong in the Lord and in his mighty power" (v. 10).

Relationships require strength. But whenever I try to love or even like someone in my own strength I am doomed to fail. We have a very limited human capacity for the type of strength we need each day. This is why we tap into the strength and power of our Lord. Another version simply says it this way, "God is strong, and he wants you strong" (MSG).

God knows we are not strong so He makes us strong. David tapped into this source of strength when he was a worshipping shepherd. Our God is almighty to make us mighty. Our Father is all-powerful to give His daughters power. God has a plan for your life and the devil has a scheme. His scheme is to knock you out of God's plan. I must warn you the devil will not fight fairly. The moment you became a daughter of God, you were marked by God's Holy Spirit and noted by the enemy. Before your rebirth you were his slave, and now you are a target. But once we are acquainted with our source of true strength, it's time to armor up. "Put on the full armor of God, so that you can take your stand against the devil's schemes" (Ephesians 6:11).

Dear Heavenly Father, I thank You that You are strong and You want me strong too. I will armor up to stand in Your plan.

I Am Strong

BECAUSE GOD IS MY SOURCE OF STRENGTH.

2

CONFIDENT
IN CHRIST

---

*The LORD's justice will dwell in the desert, his righteousness
live in the fertile field. The fruit of that righteousness will be
peace; its effect will be quietness and confidence forever.*

ISAIAH 32:16–17

When you think of an image of a confident woman, what do you imagine? In magazines, in shops, and almost every time we look at a screen, we see the world's idea of a confident woman—turning heads with her control-assured smile and impeccable style. It's no coincidence that this confidence is often for sale, in the form of a beauty or lifestyle product that will take us from a less desirable "before" to a fabulous "after." But in the long run, looking for affirmation from success or attractiveness is an empty pursuit. How many likes do we need on a photo or how many comments from strangers will it take for us to finally say, "It is enough . . . I am whole"? I promise you a million a day would never be enough to fill us.

If we trust in popularity or beauty, we'll constantly look to others to affirm our value and desirability. Our self-worth will be repeatedly jeopardized and threatened by other women, and our confidence will be fleeting. But there is another way. We have a Prince who is always willing to make beautiful the women who come to Him.

The confidence He gives us reaches deeper than we even know how to let anyone touch. It's more than just the window dressing or filter or a new accessory. It is the deep, warming glow that comes from the knowledge that we are loved and known deeply. When a woman is loved like this . . . it is seen. Christ Jesus has blessed us with His favor. It is time to allow His love to be more than enough and turn from looking elsewhere for fulfillment.

It's time to take a look at the "before and after" of our souls. It's time to truly appreciate what Christ has done and build our confidence upon it. The love He provides never fades. He longs to tenderly nurture each of us so we can blossom in His love.

Lord, thank You for renewing, cleansing, and
remaking me daily into the woman You envision.
I have confidence in Your saving grace.

I Am Strong

BECAUSE JESUS HAS GIVEN ME A TRUE
SOURCE OF CONFIDENCE.

3

NOT ALONE

No temptation has overtaken you except what is common to mankind. And God is faithful; he will not let you be tempted beyond what you can bear. But when you are tempted, he will also provide a way out so that you can endure it.

1 CORINTHIANS 10:13

Though I may never see your face or have the honor of knowing your name, I know we are not that different and in the course of life we will face many of the same challenges. Corinthians promises us that any problem we will face is not uniquely ours. We are not alone in our trials or victories. But Satan, the enemy of our souls, loves to isolate and accuse each of us as though we were. He whispers lies, "You are the only one who struggles with this. No one else is as bad as you!" I know you've heard some form of this because I, too, have heard this lie.

God does not play favorites when it comes to His promises and to His Word. He receives everyone who comes before Him with a humble and obedient heart. This is not true for the arrogant and self-righteous who imagine they have it all figured out. He hears us best when we come spent and tired of trying to do it on our own. God lifts the weary and broken and invites them: "If any of you lacks wisdom, you should ask God, who gives generously to all without finding fault, and it will be given to you" (James 1:5).

There are far too many precious women who feel alone and isolated. It is time we realized that just as we are united in our struggles, we can be united in our strength. Perhaps you have felt isolated and accused. These are lies. You are not alone. Your Lord is your redeemer rather than your accuser.

This is one of the many reasons why community is so important. When we connect with other people who have already gone through the struggle that we are presently in, we are encouraged to have faith. We step out in faith and dare to believe that just as God was faithful to them, He will be faithful to us. Allow me to assure you:

God is not angry with you.

He is not your accuser.

He is more than willing to help.

And you are not alone.

Father, I praise You that I am not alone or accused by You. Thank You for welcoming me into Your healing presence. As I am healed, I will share my journey so that others will be encouraged as well.

I Am Strong

BECAUSE I AM NOT ALONE. MY LORD IS
MY REDEEMER, NOT MY ACCUSER.

4

HEARD BY GOD

God has surely listened and has heard my prayer.
PSALM 66:19

As many parents of young children will tell you, sometimes our precious, beautiful angels hit, call names, or throw fits to get their way (not unlike us from time to time). In the heat and intensity of a battle with a two-year-old, it would appear easier for all involved to just let him have his way. Let him win this battle in hopes you will later win the war. Well, you might—but only with greater difficulty and much more struggle than the initial confrontation presented. Rewarding bad behavior always comes back to bite you in the end. Ultimately, you are not doing the child a favor but a disservice. God, our heavenly Father, is the wisest of all parents. He knows when that *thing* we are throwing a tantrum about will jeopardize something of greater value . . . our character.

I confess there have been times when I've been guilty of throwing a tantrum to get my way. I whined and complained, "God, how come they have this and I don't?" Other times it was interpersonal, "God, You know I'm right and they're wrong! Tell them or show them!" This was especially convenient in disagreements with my husband or other Christians. I imagined God interrupting their devotions to tell them how right I was. Of course, these prayers were never answered. I'm so grateful that God was after my good instead of giving me what I wanted.

There are many reasons for unanswered prayer, but never assume that He is not answering because He isn't listening. He is always actively pursuing our growth into greater good—even beyond our understanding in the moment. Whether we pray with the best of intent or with limited vision, He inclines His ear toward us, knowing exactly what we need. He has an eternal perspective in mind. As I have matured and dared to abandon myself and others into the hands of God, His righteousness prevails without my insights. We can always count on Him to listen and respond in ways that reveal His ultimate sovereignty in our lives.

Lord, I am grateful that when I speak You listen graciously, and You respond in Your will and wisdom. My future is safe in Your hands.

I Am Strong

BECAUSE I AM IN THE HANDS OF THE ONE WHO KNOWS WHAT THE FUTURE HOLDS.

5

OUR TRUE DESIRE

*I lift up my eyes to the mountains—where does
my help come from? My help comes from the
Lord, the Maker of heaven and earth.*
PSALM 121:1–2

*E*veryone is looking for fulfillment. Some may turn to money, power, or worldly success to find it. For others it is in the pursuit of love, sex, or approval. Fulfillment may even be sought in positive things, like helping people or advocating for justice. But eventually, if we're looking for fulfillment outside of God, we will end up disappointed. It is always frustrating to look for the right thing in the wrong place.

We need to lift our eyes heavenward, because our help comes from our Creator. It is only there that we will find our source and our fulfillment. Here's the sad truth: When we insist on chasing after other things, God lets us have our way. Just as He did not restrain Adam and Eve from reaching out and taking the fruit in the Garden, He does not restrain us from grasping at something to get our way. He wants to be our true desire, but He lets us have what we want, even if it is harmful to us. Paul wrote about humankind, "Furthermore, just as they did not think it worthwhile to retain the knowledge of God, so God gave them over to a depraved mind, so that they do what ought not to be done" (Romans 1:28).

When we stomp our feet and say, "No! I want what I want!" God steps back and He lets us have what our foolish will demands. It is only later that we discover it falls short of our hopes.

God doesn't want us punished any more than He wants us held captive. Listen to His open invitation: "'Come now, let us settle the matter,' says the LORD. 'Though your sins are like scarlet, they shall be as white as snow; though they are red as crimson, they shall be like wool. If you are willing and obedient, you will eat the good things of the land'" (Isaiah 1:18–19).

Let us return to Him with willing and obedient hearts and make Him our source of strength and help.

Heavenly Father, forgive me for turning to faithless things when You are my true source of life and help. Wash me clean and help me to develop a willing and obedient spirit.

I Am Strong
BECAUSE THE MAKER OF HEAVEN AND EARTH HAS MADE ME SO!

6

SATISFIED

I will be fully satisfied as with the richest of foods; with singing lips my mouth will praise you. On my bed I remember you; I think of you through the watches of the night. Because you are my help, I sing in the shadow of your wings. I cling to you; your right hand upholds me.

PSALM 63:5–8

Think of that time when you attended a banquet where there was an array of healthy, delicious foods, but you didn't overdo it. You enjoyed just enough and not too much. That night, as you drifted off to sleep, there was contentment rather than discomfort. It is deeply satisfying to be well nourished and well rested.

Our souls can experience the same kind of satisfaction that our bodies do. Just as David did, we can choose to lie in bed and remember the goodness of God. Or we can lie in bed and remember our struggles and our failures. We are encouraged to put our minds at rest by thinking about the wonders of our Father. Imagine a mighty bird sheltering and protecting its young with its wings. (From now on this is how I am going to see my Comforter!) Then as we sleep, we are at rest. In this atmosphere of gratitude and wonder, our heart sings of the Lord's help and protection in our life. Every day can be a celebration of Him.

Sleep is such a mystery. It is a time when we are truly the most vulnerable. We lose our consciousness and slip away for a few hours.

Most of us slept deeper as children than we do as adults. Content and carefree, children trade the activities of their day for the surrender of the night. As adults we have a more difficult time separating the activities of our day from our rest at night. We tend to bring the wrong things to bed with us. When we do this, we wrestle with worries and fears until the break of dawn and wake wearier than when we lay down.

I found I never slept well when I let my worries run wild before bed. Night is the time to close our eyes on the day and open our hearts to Him. Psalm 127:2 promises, "He grants sleep to those he loves." Notice it doesn't say He gives sleep to the perfect or to those who had a perfect day. He gives sleep to the children that He loves. You are that child. I want you to imagine His goodness and protection tucking you in tonight. If you do, I bet you'll wake up with a song of worship in your head in the morning.

Lord, each night I will let go of my flawed day and think about Your flawless love. You love me because You are love. Thank You for giving me sleep.

I Am Strong
WHEN I MEDITATE ON GOD'S GOODNESS AND MY SOUL FINDS REST.

7

QUIETED BY LOVE

"The LORD your God is with you, the Mighty Warrior who saves. He will take great delight in you; in his love he will no longer rebuke you, but will rejoice over you with singing."

ZEPHANIAH 3:17

S o many of us are in a sexual nightmare. Others are in relational nightmares. Some of us are in financial nightmares. I have learned that often the best way to combat a nightmare is with a dream.

For example, when my children woke in the night frightened, ill, or overly excited, I'd draw them close to quiet them. To do this, I rocked them, or lay down next to them in their beds, or if the hour was late and my husband was away, I brought them into my bed. Why? I wanted them to know I was near. It was there in my arms that I listened to their fears while I stroked their hair. I whispered affirmations of God's love and mine and reminded them of His faithful protection. I'd sing lullabies until their breathing told me they were back to sleep.

These aspects of a mother's tender response to her frightened children are drawn from the heart of God. They are but a small reflection of His desire to comfort us. When we hurt, when we fail, when we are frightened, God wants us to draw near, and never move away. As His children, we are invited to come into His arms of safety and love. There He will give us visions of beauty, capable of putting us back at ease and rest.

I love the imagery of a father tenderly rocking His daughter back to sleep so she can rest and heal. I believe with all my heart that your Father God wants to do the following for you:

- draw you near
- wash every trace of guilt and shame from you
- lay aside your fears by addressing them in the light of truth
- give you a hope and a future
- rock you until your storm is calmed
- return you to rest
- restore the dream in your heart

God isn't aloof or unapproachable. He is ready to come to our aid and with His great might saves us. He isn't annoyed when we cry out in fear or helplessness. He delights in quieting His children just as a mother considers it a joy to comfort hers. But a mother's ability to comfort has its limits, while God's ability to comfort is as limitless as His love. The depth of God's character quiets us, as He sings to us. Invite Him to draw near and quiet the storms you cannot.

Heavenly Father, I draw near to You, believing the promise of Zephaniah 3:17 that You are with me and will quiet me with Your love. The dream of this is mightier than any nightmare I now face. I surrender to resting in You.

I Am Strong

BECAUSE THE MIGHTY ONE IS WITH ME, SINGING AND QUIETING MY SOUL WITH HIS LOVE.

KEPT SAFE

Above all else, guard your heart, for everything you do flows from it.
PROVERBS 4:23

What is the most valuable thing in your home? What would happen if it was stolen or lost? You might be able to replace the item with savings or insurance—which is a hassle to be sure, but not a total disaster. Now, what is the most priceless item in your house emotionally? Perhaps, like me, it's a photo album, or another item that tells the story of a time past. If this was taken from your home, it would be nearly impossible to replace. You would have to accept its loss. You'd be sad, but life would go on. The truth is that if a thief broke into your home and stole everything of value, he wouldn't have taken the most valuable thing—because he could not steal your most precious treasure . . . your heart.

In fact, the only way a heart can be stolen is if you have attached it to someone or something else that can steal it. Then your loss could be truly great. This is the reason God tells us to love Him with our entire hearts—because in Him alone our hearts are kept safe. Your heart, or "affections," as one Bible version puts it, has the power to "influence everything else in your life" (Proverbs 4:23 TLB).

The verse that tells us to guard our hearts also describes it as a "wellspring." A wellspring is a source of clean, fresh, safe water that nourishes the life of the plants and animals surrounding it. It certainly influences everything around it. Civilization tends to spring up around water sources. In arid places, the spring is literally the difference between life and death. If it is contaminated somehow, or if it is cut off from its source deep within the earth, everything in the area is affected. Things wither and die. So a wellspring is worth guarding and caring for, protecting from pollution, and maintaining its connection to the source.

We guard our hearts as if they are providing life-giving springs of water to our lives. We guard them from being poisoned by pollution when we keep them from bitterness and offense. We guard them from drought by staying connected to the true source through prayer and praise. We guard them from unhealthy affections by not attaching them to unreliable things of this world that can steal our hearts away. When you diligently guard your heart, loving the "Lord your God with all your heart and with all your soul and with all your mind," as Jesus commanded, He will keep you safe and flourishing (Matthew 22:37).

God, show me how to give my whole heart to You and to guard it well. I know it is safest in Your care.

I Am Strong
BECAUSE I GUARD THE WELLSPRING OF MY HEART.

9

BE STILL

"Be still, and know that I am God."
PSALM 46:10

Tonight, as you go to sleep, I want you to try an experiment. Build in time in your normal bedtime routine to lie in the silence and open your heart to God. Accept the invitation to simply revere God, to be still and know. Know what? Know Him as God by allowing Him to reveal Himself in the midst of your life—in your joys as well as your pains, conflicts, or crises. He wants to whisper words of love to you before sleep overtakes you.

In the quiet stillness say nothing . . . just listen. If you're in the middle of a conflict don't justify your position. Be still and allow God to reveal Himself in your silence. You'll gain His insight and perspective as you lay down all arguments.

Prayer and meditation are much more about what we hear than what we say. When we think of prayer, we often think of it as something we produce—words we say, the outpourings of our hearts, our petitions laid out before Him. All these are good. But that's not all there is. Yes, there is a time to ask Him for what our hearts desire. There is a time to plead for justice, and to beseech Him. But rivers of our own words will not wash us clean. They merely express our point of view. My wild torrent of reasoning is much too muddy and troubled to cleanse; it only stirs up things and deposits additional debris. I need to draw my insight from the deep waters that have the power to refresh and remove my guilt and shame.

Pause. *Selah*. Make the time to hear what your God is saying. If worries and tumultuous thoughts crowd your mind at the end of the day, you don't have to let them sap your strength and disturb your rest. Don't lie there and watch endless replays of the stresses and failures of the day. Instead, reclaim a moment of silence to be with the One who can bring true peace. Only He can truly set you free from the thoughts that wear you down and replenish your soul as you sleep. When you wake, you will discover that "because of the LORD's great love we are not consumed, for his compassions never fail. They are new every morning; great is your faithfulness" (Lamentations 3:22–23).

Father, as I go to sleep, still my soul and speak to my heart. Only You can stop my racing thoughts. I give the final moments of my day to You, in thanks for the new mercies You have in store for me in the morning.

I Am Strong

WHEN I AM STILL AND QUIET BEFORE MY GOD.

Strong in
Spirit

THE POWER OF SONG

Sing to the LORD a new song, for he has done marvelous things;
his right hand and his holy arm have worked salvation for him.

PSALM 98:1

There is a beautiful and divine connection between love and music. They expand and reveal one another. Music has the power to transport us. Words immersed in music have the power to touch places in our hearts that nothing else can reach. All of us have found ourselves swept into an ecstasy of great joy or lowered into the depths of sorrow by the power of a song.

Music is an essential key to the awakening of our love for God, because it has the power to usher us past our present reality and into the very presence of God. It lifts our truest and deepest emotions closer to the surface and transports us to a dimension closer to the heart of God. It can speak for us when words are hard to express and our feelings are overwhelming.

Did you know there is an anointing on music? Therefore, you must choose it wisely. In the Old Testament, the anointing was most often associated with the pouring forth of oil on a king, priest, or prophet. It was a tangible representation of God's Spirit. In the New Testament, the anointing represented the indwelling and empowerment of the Holy Spirit to reveal Christ. So godly, anointed music is empowered by the Spirit to draw us into His presence. There have been times of worship when I've been utterly overcome by His presence. Though I did not see Him with my eyes, it was as though He encompassed my entire being. In that presence, I felt completely safe and loved.

Because music has the power to take us places emotionally, it is important we choose our destinations wisely. If you desire to walk in purity, you must guard against any unwanted influence. Music will bypass your first line of defense and take up residence in your mind . . . even if you don't want it to. You might never have personally sung the lyrics, but there it is anyway, repeating its message over and over in your head. We've all heard people complain, "I have that song stuck in my head!"

So replace those impure songs by singing another, a heavenly song. Not all songs of earth are bad, but not all will draw you closer to God. The songs of heaven will. As we sing these songs, we proclaim our love and desire for God. This is a form of worship, and worship always empowers the worshipper with a greater revelation of the object of her desire. You can use the power of music to bask in God's presence; it cannot help but draw you closer to Him.

Lord, thank You for the gift of music. Be near me when I lift my heart in song, and show me how to use the power of music to strengthen my soul. May every song in my heart glorify You.

I Am Strong

WHEN I RAISE MY VOICE TO
SING A HEAVENLY SONG.

2

CONFIDENT AND COMPETENT

Such confidence we have through Christ before God. Not that we are competent in ourselves to claim anything for ourselves, but our competence comes from God.

2 CORINTHIANS 3:4–5

I am not sure there is a single area in my life where I feel completely confident and competent. On my own I am confident that I am incompetent. The good news is we don't have to be. God is the one who makes us competent. No one can lead a life of faith without the leading of the Holy Spirit. King David prayed, "Create in me a pure heart, O God, and renew a steadfast spirit within me. Do not cast me from your presence or take your Holy Spirit from me" (Psalm 51:10–11).

David knew who his source was for a clean heart, and he understood the involvement of the Holy Spirit in that process. In John 20, Jesus imparted the Holy Spirit to His disciples. They needed the Holy Spirit so they could forgive. Second Corinthians 3:6 reads, "He has made us competent as ministers of a new covenant—not of the letter but of the Spirit; for the letter kills, but the Spirit gives life." Why not invite the Holy Spirit to breathe upon the Scriptures you encounter so they bring forth life and transformation?

The Holy Spirit is the promised Comforter and Counselor who will teach and remind us of everything Jesus said. This precious gift means we have a Tutor as we study the Word and a Guide as we pursue His heart. The Spirit opens our eyes that we might see, our ears that we might hear, and our hearts that we might believe.

Heavenly Father, I thank You that I am competent and confident in You. Holy Spirit, lead me and create a clean heart and a renewed, right spirit within me. Empower me to live in such a way that my life glorifies the Father.

I Am Strong

BECAUSE CHRIST MAKES ME CONFIDENT AND COMPETENT.

3

A HEALTHY HEART

A cheerful heart is good medicine, but a crushed spirit dries up the bones.

PROVERBS 17:22

The Bible gives us amazing insight into the source of our health. Moisture is found in the marrow or center of the bones. This is where the immune system and the blood cells are fortified. Our life is in the blood, and our blood is fortified from the marrow in our bones. If the bones dry up, the very source of our life is compromised. This is confirmed again in Proverbs 14:29–30: "Whoever is patient has great understanding, but one who is quick-tempered displays folly. A heart at peace gives life to the body, but envy rots the bones."

The Bible contrasts patience with a quick temper and peace with envy. Patience gives understanding, while a quick temper is evidence of folly. A peaceful heart gives life to a body, while envy or ill will corrupts or rots your very bones. Isn't it amazing that some forms of cancer are treated by a bone marrow transplant? The health of our bone marrow is so crucial. Bones are the structural support of our bodies. They are the frame by which we stand and without which we fall.

The Bible confirms there is a real and ever-present relationship between the spiritual heart and health. I am not implying that those who are sick have an underlying spiritual problem. We live in a fallen world that is riddled by the curse of sickness and disease. What I am saying is that bitterness, unforgiveness, unresolved anger, and other heart issues directly affect your immune system. In his book Make Anger Your Ally, Neil Clark Warren reported that resentment is most frequently connected with punishing ailments, and frustration is a close second. He lists a sampling of these common ailments brought on by unresolved anger: headaches, stomach problems, colds, colitis, and hypertension.

Other studies have included afflictions ranging from types of arthritis, various respiratory ailments, skin disease, neck and back problems, to even cancer. The Bible has already declared for centuries what man is now finding to be true. Proverbs 3:5–8 is a wealth of wisdom concerning how we should live:

> Trust in the LORD with all your heart and lean not on your own understanding; in all your ways submit to him, and he will make your paths straight. Do not be wise in your own eyes; fear the LORD and shun evil. This will bring health to your body and nourishment to your bones.

We have a promise here. If we live according to God's divine health plan, He says it brings health to our bodies and nourishment to our bones.

Lord, You connected my heart and my health on purpose. Please help me live with a healthy spirit, so I can avoid needless physical consequences. Help me keep both body and soul nourished on Your wisdom.

I Am Strong

WHEN I KEEP A CHEERFUL, HEALTHY HEART.

4

EMBRACING A WOMAN'S NATURE

Instead, speaking the truth in love, we will grow to become in every respect the mature body of him who is the head, that is, Christ.

EPHESIANS 4:15

As women, our very nature and physical design are set up with nurture and tenderness in mind. We are not constructed with hard edges but gentle curves. We were created with a greater capacity for tenderness and compassion than men. We feel both love and pain deeper within our being. We are more empathetic than males and can be moved to tears over the pain, struggles, and losses of total strangers. When we are not allowed to express these emotions in a valid way, we run the risk of exploding either outwardly or inwardly.

What happens when we explode? Two of my least favorite Scriptures tell us how it plays out in the context of a marriage. This was often quoted to me in my newlywed days: "Better to live on a corner of the roof than share a house with a quarrelsome wife" (Proverbs 25:24). Or the other even less attractive version: "Better to live in a desert than with a quarrelsome and nagging wife" (Proverbs 21:19).

Ouch. Life on the corner of a roof would mean being exposed to the extremes of all the elements. The roof provides no shelter from rain, snow, wind, or the harsh sun. Solomon was telling us it is better to live under these conditions than shelter in a house with a quarrelsome woman. I used to argue with my husband, John, that back then they used the roof as a type of alternative to the porch, but I found the reemphasis of this Scripture hard to explain away. Better to live in the desert or wilderness with the serpents and scorpions than with an angry, grumpy, and argumentative woman. Warring becomes wearing . . . not only on others but also on ourselves.

Women are created to be healthy and passionate, loving and compassionate. When we go against our original design or purpose for creation, we actually war physically against our bodies. We violate the life-giving, strengthening, and supportive role in our lives. Women can fulfill this role whether they are married or single.

When we are tempted to bottle up our thoughts and emotions to the point of explosion, let us remember that this doesn't do anyone any good. It doesn't save us from conflict; it only results in an internal ill-temper that hurts us and everyone around us. Let us speak the truth in love, in a manner that can be heard, and live in harmony with the healthy, passionate, loving nature we were given by God.

Lord, give me an accurate vision of my nature as a woman.
Teach me to be gentle, yet strong, serving You and using
the voice You gave me to speak the truth in love.

I Am Strong

WHEN I EMBRACE AND CELEBRATE MY NATURE, SPEAKING THE TRUTH IN LOVE.

5

CALM AND POWERFUL

A gentle answer turns away wrath, but a harsh word stirs up anger.

O ften I can remember the turning point of a conversation when it went from good to bad or from bad to good. At times, I could hear the Holy Spirit warn me: "Stay calm, lower your voice, answer gently. Don't say what you want to say, but listen to My still, small voice and speak My words instead." Sometimes I am obedient and listen . . . Other times I just try to sneak in one more comment before obeying and find out just how costly my foolishness is.

I have found the secret to being heard. It really is quite simple: If you want to be heard, say it the way you would want to hear it. My children, my husband, my employees, my dog, everyone, in fact, listens more when I say things the way I want to hear them. I know I prefer to be spoken to in a gentle, respectful tone. I hear so much better when I am not being yelled at. It is not the volume level or the repetition of words that grabs the attention, respect, and commitment of others. It is the importance of what we speak and the tone in which it is delivered. No one takes a person seriously if they are throwing a fit. Oh, they may get their way for the moment, but it will cost them later. We throw fits and raise our voices for many reasons. Here are a few:

1. We are afraid we are not being heard.
2. Yelling has produced results (getting our way) in the past.
3. We want to intimidate or control others.
4. It is what we lived as a child.
5. We are still angry over an unresolved issue.
6. It's a bad habit.

Most of these reasons are rooted in fear. God has not given us a spirit of fear but of power, love, and a sound mind (2 Timothy 1:7). We will yell and throw fits when we feel powerless. We will seek to intimidate and control others when we are self-serving. We will revert to our past when perfected love has not yet cast out fear. We will overreact whenever we have carried the weight of yesterday's issues into today.

As we renew our mind, bad habits are broken and the tyranny of fear is thwarted. I found out a long time ago that no matter how things appear, I am not in control of them. I can control myself, but God is ultimately in control of everything.

Accepting this truth puts us in the right state of mind to communicate in such a way that lets us be heard.

Lord, when I struggle and fight to maintain control, help me remember that at the very least I can control my tongue and my tone. By Your grace make me sensitive to Your still, small voice and allow it to guide me.

I Am Strong

WHEN I SPEAK IN A CALM AND POWERFUL WAY.

6

PASSIONATE

"[Sin] desires to have you, but you must rule over it."
GENESIS 4:7

Too frequently our culture limits passion to the confines of the sexual, but passion encompasses a much broader spectrum. It's tricky to define because it embraces both extremes of human emotion: love and hate. Passion is closely associated with emotion, enthusiasm, excitement, desire, fondness, love, affection. Who wouldn't want more of these? On the other hand, it's also associated with words that can bind us, like infatuation, craving, and lust. And then on the next level, it's associated with words like outburst, fury, anger, indignation, rage, resentment, and wrath.

Between these extremes of love and hate, how can we live a passionate life without getting burned?

We can take our cue from one of the first stories ever told about passion gone wrong: the story of Cain and Abel in Genesis 4. God accepted Abel's wholehearted sacrifice, but He rejected Cain's half-hearted sacrifice. And Cain was enraged. When God saw Cain was enflamed with anger toward his brother, "The LORD said to Cain, 'Why are you angry? Why is your face downcast? If you do what is right, will you not be accepted? But if you do not do what is right, sin is crouching at your door; it desires to have you, but you must rule over it'" (Genesis 4:6–7).

Sadly, Cain did not make things right with God. Rather than master sin and rule over his anger, he murdered his brother.

God's warning to Cain is also a warning to us. Yes, we are probably not to the point of murder, but "if we do not do what is right," sin is just as surely crouching at our door. We must rule over our emotions and focus them constructively rather than destructively.

The truth is, passion can be a valuable indicator, no matter which end of the spectrum it is on. Passion displays itself as a heightened physical and emotional state of preparedness to defend something about which we are . . . passionate. We tend to be passionate about what is important to us. Most of us are not easily worked up by the trivial unless it ties into something meaningful to us on a grander scale. So when our passions are aroused they reveal what's important to us. We can choose to funnel that energy toward life instead of letting it descend into the realm of chaos like Cain did. Even amid emotional extremes, we have the power of choice. It is within our ability to govern our passions and make choices that lead to life.

Father, teach me to listen to the passions in my life and to bring them to You to be sanctified. Please align what is important to me with what is important to You.

I Am Strong

BECAUSE I CAN CHOOSE TO RULE MY SOUL RATHER THAN ALLOW MY PASSIONS TO HAVE FULL REIGN.

7

WORSHIP IS MORE THAN A SONG

Be filled with the Spirit, speaking to one another
with psalms, hymns, and songs from the Spirit. Sing
and make music from your heart to the Lord.

EPHESIANS 5:18–19

Praise and worship is more than a spiritual discipline—it is a passion, a pleasure, and a key to falling deeper in love with God. You draw closer to God by listening to and singing love songs to and about Him.

In today's verse, we find an admonishment to be filled with the Spirit during praise and worship. We are filled as we sing out loud and make music in our hearts, but this verse introduces another key as well . . . our communication about God with others. Worship is more than singing. It reveals itself in our conversations because it is only natural to converse about what our heart overflows with. When you love someone you talk about them. It is exciting to be loved, and of course you would want to share the beauty of that with others.

Friends share common bonds, and a shared passion is like friends standing around a campfire, all freely enjoying its warmth and beauty. This bond causes us to build one another up in truth. This is why corporate worship is so powerful; you are expressing your love for God while surrounded by friends.

True friends lift one another higher and challenge each other to walk in a manner pleasing to our Lord. When your friends follow Jesus, you're all heading in the same direction. Surround yourself with those who are one with you in spirit and purpose. You won't always agree on everything. Be teachable and protective of your bond.

Be filled with the Spirit and worship—in your conversation, in song, and in the community of believers.

Dear Lord, let words and songs of praise flow out of my life. Overwhelm me with Your love until I cannot stay quiet about how amazing it is to be loved by You.

I Am Strong

BECAUSE I AM STRENGTHENED BY A LIFESTYLE OF WORSHIP.

8

SPIRITUAL AUTHORITY

For the Spirit God gave us does not make us timid,
but gives us power, love and self-discipline.

2 TIMOTHY 1:7

The Holy Spirit imparts power, love, and self-discipline to us. The combination of these three virtues cannot help but yield strong women. I am convinced that the gifts God has placed in our individual lives will not flourish without these gifts of the Spirit in operation. Another version of this verse reads, "For God has not given us a spirit of fear, but of power and of love and of a sound mind" (2 Timothy 1:7 NKJV).

I don't know of anything that shuts down our power, love, and soundness of mind more than a spirit of fear. One reason is that fear torments us with questions that undermine those three attributes. First let's talk about the aspect of power. Another way of saying this would be spiritual authority. We have little to no power or authority in and of ourselves. Adam had yielded the dominion that God had granted him and Eve in the garden. Through obedience, Jesus took back what had been lost through Adam's disobedience. "Then Jesus came to them and said, 'All authority in heaven and on earth has been given to me'" (Matthew 28:18).

Our authority and power are realized in Christ. Why would we fear if we have hidden our lives in Him?

In Second Timothy, Paul encourages Timothy, a young minister and disciple of Jesus, to grow the gift of faith in his life. We know this because in the previous verse Paul reminds him, "For this reason I remind you to fan into flame the gift of God, which is in you through the laying on of my hands" (2 Timothy 1:6).

Whether or not someone has laid hands on you, we each have been given a measure of faith that is ours to multiply by tending it. The topic of faith is mentioned nearly 300 times in the New Testament. One of the most arresting declarations concerning faith is found in the book of Hebrews: "And without faith it is impossible to please God, because anyone who comes to him must believe that he exists and that he rewards those who earnestly seek him" (11:6).

Most of us believe that God exists. Where we get tripped up is believing that He will reward those who earnestly seek Him. Fear will attack the strongest of us with its accusations. *You are not doing enough. You are not powerful enough. You are not loving enough. You are not enough.* Because of Jesus we answer back that in Christ we are more than enough.

Heavenly Father, thank You for giving me Your Holy Spirit who reminds me that in Christ I can walk in love, authority, and in peace and clarity of mind.

I Am Strong

BECAUSE IN CHRIST I HAVE BEEN GIVEN POWER, LOVE, AND SOUNDNESS OF MIND.

9

PRAY ACCORDING TO THE SPIRIT

And pray in the Spirit on all occasions with all kinds of prayers and requests. With this in mind, be alert and always keep on praying for all the Lord's people.

EPHESIANS 6:18

Prayer and obedience are the most powerful tools in spiritual warfare and we are in a season of high alert. Notice Paul suggests that we pray in the Spirit not just sometimes but on all occasions. How do we pray according to the Spirit? One way is to pray the Word of God. When you read through the Scriptures you will find there are as many different prayers as there are needs. The "Our Father" is a good daily prayer, but as we move through the day we will discover all sorts of things to pray about. We will see people in need, nations in crisis, leaders who need wisdom and insight. We should pray for our friends, our families, and our enemies.

Another way to pray in the Spirit is to listen to the leading of the Holy Spirit as you pray. There will be times when you will sense something is wrong or someone is in need. Pray for them. So many times I will reach out later and find out they were going through a rough time.

Prayer can be formal and informal. You can pray standing, sitting, lying down, or kneeling. Prayer can be as loud as a shout or a silent meditation of your heart. Prayer should be as natural as breathing. We are encouraged to "rejoice always, pray continually, give thanks in all circumstances; for this is God's will for you in Christ Jesus" (1 Thessalonians 5:16–18).

Saint Augustine said it this way, "Pray as though everything depended on God and work as though everything depended on you."

We are only as powerful as our prayers. Strong women are careful to keep their prayer connection strong. I like to pray as I listen to worship music. I also like to keep a journal of my prayers; over the decades they have become testaments to God's faithfulness.

Our heavenly Father knew the battles that we would face and He supplied everything we would need to not only stand, but to overcome. The enemy will continue to fight us, but he will not win.

Heavenly Father, teach me to pray until it is as natural as speaking. Thank You for the leading of Your Holy Spirit.

I Am Strong
WHEN MY PRAYERS ARE STRONG.

Strong in
Purity

PURE

*To him who is able to keep you from stumbling and to
present you blameless before the presence of his glory
with great joy, to the only God, our Savior, through
Jesus Christ our Lord, be glory, majesty, dominion, and
authority, before all time and now and forever. Amen.*

JUDE 24–25 ESV

We are not able to keep ourselves pure, but He is. At first glance, purity may seem to be the same as holiness, but it is not. Holiness means to be set apart or consecrated, whereas purity is how we conduct ourselves because we have been consecrated. Purity is the by-product of holiness. We learn to conduct ourselves in purity by constructing a foundation built on the living Word of God.

God wants to be our life source. If you are truly brave, invite the Holy Spirit to examine your heart and motives by the light of God's piercing and penetrating Word. Hebrews 4:12–13 says:

> For the word of God is alive and active. Sharper than any double-edged
> sword, it penetrates even to dividing soul and spirit, joints and marrow;
> it judges the thoughts and attitudes of the heart. Nothing in all creation is
> hidden from God's sight. Everything is uncovered and laid bare before the
> eyes of him to whom we must give account.

Trust me, this is not for the faint of heart. God's Word is not merely letters on paper . . . it's alive. If you want the real strength that comes from embracing truth, I dare you to believe His Word and draw near. His living Word longs to dance in your heart and whisper to you in the night. It is so sharp it can separate the soul from the spirit, and in the process, reveal hidden thoughts and attitudes.

Remember, nothing is hidden from God. He sees it all, even though we cannot. Often our hearts deceive us, but if we ask for truth, God will share His discernment with us through His Word. We don't want the counsel of man . . . We want the wisdom and insight of God. The counsel of man is always influenced by the culture and standards of this age. It is foolishness that readjusts itself every decade or so, reflecting the moral temperature of society. But God's Word stands forever, and it is the standard to which we will give an account.

You will be confronted with truths and promises in the Bible that may initially seem impossible or unrealistic . . . but they are not. As we take in the Word, we'll learn that purity and holiness are possible. Because God's call to holiness is not about rules; it's about being His.

Heavenly Father, I invite Your Word to be living and active in my life. You are the One who makes me holy, so separate me from the lies that say purity is impossible. I want to live in such a way that others know that I am Yours.

I Am Strong

BECAUSE GOD'S WORD IS LIVING
AND ACTIVE IN MY LIFE.

2

DEVOTED

I am jealous for you with a godly jealousy. I promised you to one husband, to Christ, so that I might present you as a pure virgin to him. But I am afraid that just as Eve was deceived by the serpent's cunning, your minds may somehow be led astray from your sincere and pure devotion to Christ.

2 CORINTHIANS 11:2-3

I am passionate to see the power of purity reign in the life of every woman, whether she is single or married, young or old. When we talk about purity in the church, often we are talking about sexual choices and behavior, but purity as referenced in today's verse refers to our internal "pure devotion to Christ." Purity starts in our minds. And the fight for purity includes refusing to be led astray by the deceiver. This means searching the Word for truth and inviting the power of the Holy Spirit into your heart to separate truth from falsehood.

As Paul points out in today's verse, we may be led astray from our pure devotion to Christ. We can choose whose words we will listen to: the words of our Savior or the words of the tempter who seeks our life. It is the Word of God that is the ultimate authority. If you ask God, He will take the sword of the Spirit and cut away every falsehood from your life.

If enough pressure is applied to us in any given situation, we will eventually falter in any battle that we have not already won inwardly. Let's start with purity of thought. As we take every thought captive and make it obedient to Christ (2 Corinthians 10:5), we will see purity flow into every area of life.

Dear Heavenly Father, You are the very essence of purity and holiness. I am Yours, and I commit to take in Your Word, allowing it honor, preeminence, and authority in every area of my life. I invite the sword of Your Word to sever every unhealthy and ungodly entanglement, to purify me from the inside out.

I Am Strong

BECAUSE I SEEK PURITY LIKE A TREASURE, DRAWING STRENGTH FROM THE UNADULTERATED WORDS OF CHRIST.

3

THE PACKAGE

"People look at the outward appearance, but the LORD looks at the heart."
1 SAMUEL 16:7

You may look at today's verse and argue that appearance shouldn't matter, because God looks at the heart. Well, thank heavens He looks at our hearts, but we do still live on the earth, and everyone here looks at the exterior and is moved by what they see.

We're exhorted to be careful of the way we package ourselves. We have been warned vanity is a fleeting hope, and it is therefore foolish to trust in our looks. But just because we don't trust in them doesn't mean we should neglect them.

The fact is, we are always communicating, whether we intend to or not. Our messages will go out through one of three channels: what we say (our words and tone), what we do (our manners and actions), and what we look like (our visual appearances or presentation). And people are often more influenced by what they see than by what they hear.

When we understand this, we can use this to our advantage and communicate our intentions effectively. I am certain that you've heard one form or another the old adage, "You never get a second chance to make a good first impression." Well, it may be old, but it was certainly never truer. There have never been so many options for expression, but what exactly are we saying?

How you dress and present yourself not only sends an immediate message to others, but it may imply more than you intended. It may betray what you really think of yourself. Or what you trust in. Or where you think your influence comes from. Or, of course, to whom you belong.

I'm not about to give you specific fashion advice, for only you can answer: What are you presently communicating? What message are you sending? Is it an accurate reflection of who you are, or are you just posing and posting?

Let's say your outward dress and appearance accurately reflect who you are. You may say, "I am a professional, and my dress is appropriate for my profession." Or you might be a student and feel your style of dress reflects that well. But let's dig a little deeper. How are you affecting others by your manner of clothing? Do people see you or only what you are wearing? When others look at you, what do they see?

While we should never trust in our looks, we can use this form of communication in a wise and godly manner, just as we do with our words and deeds.

Lord, show me how to be wise in all forms of communication—including how I present myself. Reveal to me what I am really saying with my appearance, and let it all be to Your glory.

I Am Strong

BECAUSE I AM THE WHOLE
PACKAGE—INWARDLY AND
OUTWARDLY DEVOTED TO GOD.

4

WOVEN IN WONDER

"Before I formed you in the womb I knew you."
JEREMIAH 1:5

God is intimately involved in our formation. He wove us in the womb long before our mother could sense our presence. Before we could even have the capacity to know ourselves . . . He knew us. While we grew in secret He planned out the days of our lives and stretched before us our path of destiny. You were never merely a clump of cells; you were always alive in Him.

Every child born is a gift of hope, entrusted to our care. If you have ever witnessed the miracle of a human birth then you know that each baby is wrapped in the wonder of potential.

I remember that before I even knew I was pregnant with my third son I felt his life quicken in me. John was ministering in Rochester, New York, and during the worship service I found myself feeling unusually weak. I felt myself swoon, so I sat down. As I took my seat I heard the Holy Spirit whisper, "You carry life . . . Within you grows a son." At that same moment I felt overwhelmed by God's presence. That is just one example of how intimately acquainted God is with babies growing in the womb.

But what if you were never told this? What if no one ever told you that you were woven in wonder and known by your Creator? What if instead you heard things that implied you were an accident or a mistake? If we fail to realize the wonder involved in our own creation, then it will be difficult for us to recognize the wonder in others. If we were raised to feel as if *we* were a bother, then it would be easy to see a child as an intrusion.

Far too many women feel pressured to balance everything—careers, motherhood, extra activities— because our culture of capitalism has stripped motherhood of its value. In many ways, life is a test of time. You can have a career, but it's a challenge to balance a career and be a present mother. My children have brought me more joy and opportunity for growth than any career achievement. If you want to be a mother, don't be ashamed. It will require more of you than you could ever imagine, but at the same time, it will give back more than you could ever dream.

Heavenly Father, You are the giver of life. I believe You wove me in wonder and laid out my days with a smile. You have entrusted mothers with a noble task because children are a gift from You.

I Am Strong

BECAUSE I WAS MADE FOR HIM AND BY HIM.

5

SOUL TIES

"Do not think that I have come to bring peace to the earth.
I have not come to bring peace, but a sword."

MATTHEW 10:34 ESV

Jesus wants to set each of us free from anything that keeps us from Him. Spiritual warfare involves confronting any idol or obstacle that stands in the way of our relationship with Him.

I believe that we can confront areas of captivity. When Jesus saw chains, He broke them; when Jesus saw demons, He drove them out; when Jesus saw people inflicted and sick, He healed them; when Jesus saw people bound by sin, He forgave them and then empowered them to go and sin no more. I love Jesus because He is so real, relevant, and practical.

I came to realize that I was suffering from the bondage of unhealthy soul ties that needed severing. What is a soul tie? In simple terms, it is when our souls become knit to another. Now this can be both a good and a bad thing. A mother's soul is knit to her infant's. But as he grows and becomes a man, his relationship with his mother must change so that he can give his heart to his wife. A husband's soul should be knit to his bride's so that the two may become one flesh. These are good and healthy ties that bind and knit our hearts together in love. Healthy ties like this can also be forged in friendships, like David and Jonathan's. Yours may be with a sister or close friend. There is an unspoken knowing between you.

But when unhealthy soul ties form, there is control and fear rather than union and fellowship. These can be formed through illicit sex, unhealthy dependences, or dysfunctional or abusive relationships. Unhealthy soul ties leave us broken. Often we try to untie them, but I have learned that it is better to allow the Lord to pass His sword and sever what binds us. Only God can restore our brokenness to wholeness.

We have a faithful and compassionate High Priest who knows you intimately. He is willing to use His sword to sever anything that holds you back from Him. He wants every unhealthy soul tie severed so only what is healthy will remain. He will send His Word to heal and restore your soul. Set aside some time for prayer to allow God to accomplish His purification of your life. Ask the Holy Spirit to reveal any unhealthy soul tie and then invite His Word sword to cut it. He who promises is faithful.

Lord, please reveal any unhealthy soul ties in my life,
and break them with the power of Your Holy Spirit.
Heal me and restore my soul. Show me how to nurture
the good ties in my life and keep them healthy.

I Am Strong

BECAUSE I HAVE BOUND
MY SOUL TO THE TRUTH.

6

HEALING REGRET

For you created my inmost being; you knit me together in my mother's womb. I praise you because I am fearfully and wonderfully made; your works are wonderful, I know that full well. My frame was not hidden from you when I was made in the secret place, when I was woven together in the depths of the earth. Your eyes saw my unformed body; all the days ordained for me were written in your book before one of them came to be. How precious to me are your thoughts, God! How vast is the sum of them!
PSALM 139:13–17

Here David captures a detailed poetic account of every life that graces the womb. But what if you have experienced the pain of abortion? If so, I need to speak healing to you. You may have been a frightened daughter who believed a lie, or perhaps you lost a grandchild. Whatever the circumstance and whoever you are, I believe God the Father is saying: You're forgiven, and a life waits for you on the other side.

Abortions are rarely mourned openly. The beauty of those little lives is swept away neatly and efficiently. It is only afterwards that the shroud of guilt and shame covers the mother, father, and anyone else involved.

We live in a culture that is overwhelmingly selfish. It can never empower you to live in godliness, because it is governed by the demands of self. We also navigate the challenge of churches that are harsh on or judgmental of unmarried pregnant women. I recently sat on a panel where two of the five Christian women present had had abortions because they couldn't face the judgment and shame of the church. Women seeking abortions hear a very different narrative from society:

"You're young and beautiful . . . your whole life is ahead of you."
"Someday you'll make a wonderful mother, but today is not
     that time."
"You can have children when you are ready."
"This baby is not wanted, and every child deserves to be wanted."

I have heard from women young and old who listened to this kind of advice and lived to regret it. They went into the clinic as two people and came out fractured and broken. Shouldn't we who have known the love and mercy of Jesus be more supportive than the abortion clinics? Pro-life is not a voting stance; it is a lifestyle that supports adoptions and courageous choices.

No matter how painful the regret, we can never go back and change what happened. Our hope is in looking ahead. You must embrace God's truth and forgiveness. If you've had an abortion, forgive yourself and let the healing begin.

Heavenly Father, show me how to be an instrument of healing rather than
of judgment. I want to see the beauty and value of life the way You do.

I Am Strong

BECAUSE I CHOOSE LIFE AND HOPE
OVER REGRET AND SHAME.

7

HONORING MARRIAGE

Marriage should be honored by all, and the marriage bed kept pure,
for God will judge the adulterer and all the sexually immoral.

HEBREWS 13:4

To tackle this verse, we must first have a better understanding of the word honor. We honor something or someone when we add a greater weight or value to what it is or who they are. For example, I honor my husband when I speak respectfully and work with him rather than against him. On the other hand, when you dishonor someone or something, you are careless and reckless because you do not value them or it. In marriages, husbands can dishonor their wives just as wives can dishonor their husbands by not understanding this principle of honor. The verse in Hebrews speaks specifically about honoring the "marriage bed" or place of intimacy.

We honor our marriage before the wedding by remaining pure. Sex outside of marriage dishonors the covenant of marriage, the individuals involved in the act, and God. Conversely, sex within the covenant of marriage honors God, the individuals, and their marriage. Another way we honor our marriage is by never allowing other people or things into our places of intimacy. This means we do not involve ourselves in that which detracts from the beauty of exclusive sexual union. Some of these detractors are pornography, masturbation, perversion, prostitution, or impurity.

Because I did not live these truths before I was married, I had to face off with many shadow places once I was married. I should have been able to give myself freely to my husband, but I found myself bound to the choices of my past.

We are created to be united sexually with only one person because sexual intimacy is reserved for the union of two who become one through the covenant of marriage. Intimacy must be exclusive for it to be intimate. If we choose to have sex with many it degrades what is special about the one.

I believe this is one reason why adultery in its many forms is rampant in our culture. Because we don't understand the concept of covenant, people say, "Marriage is just a piece of paper." Marriage is not merely two people becoming one; it is God making the two one. If we do not understand that marriage includes three, not one, then all it becomes is . . . paper.

Honoring God's Word brings strength, covenant, and intimacy to marriage. God is in the process of restoring what has been torn and healing what has been dishonored.

Heavenly Father, teach me how to honor marriage. Holy Spirit, reveal any area of defilement and dishonor when it comes to my marriage or my view of marriage. (This can be prayed whether you are single or married.) I want to honor Your covenant of intimacy in my life.

I Am Strong

WHEN I GUARD INTIMACY AND
REJECT WHAT VIOLATES A
COVENANT OF MARRIAGE.

8

PROTECTED

The LORD is my rock, my fortress and my deliverer.

PSALM 18:2

was shaken. Our pastor had just asked me to speak to a group of girls about sexual purity, and I had no idea what I was going to say to them. Not only was I clueless, I was borderline terrified. What was wrong with me? For years I'd traveled all over the world speaking in front of large groups of women of all ages. Why was I afraid of our local high school youth group girls? I took a deep breath. I just needed to get a hold of myself. After all, I was a former youth pastor's wife. I'd survived those two years more or less unscathed. Then I realized it wasn't the age group that bothered me . . . it was the subject matter. I knew they would ask me what they could and couldn't do within their relationships with boys.

What was I going to say to a bunch of high school girls about "limits"? I didn't even have a daughter, and I had almost no time to prepare.

I hit the floor and prayed. *Father, I really need an answer for these girls. I want to impart Your wisdom, not my opinion or that of someone else. And I really need to know soon.*

I waited. Nothing. I got up off the floor and headed for the shower. Tomorrow was D-Day. As I showered, my mind wandered, until I heard the Holy Spirit speak and focus my direction: "You are looking for rules to restrict their behavior. Rules will not keep them. The empowerment they need must be born out of relationship. Don't tell them what they 'can't' do; tell them what they 'can.' Tell them they can go as far with their boyfriends as they are comfortable with in front of their fathers!"

There was my answer. Fathers should be the protectors of their daughter's virtue. Maybe that is not the case for you. Perhaps you do not have an earthly father to protect you. The good news is you do have a heavenly one. He would never want to see you used or violated. Perhaps you've already gone too far. Regardless of your past He is watching over your future. This answer doesn't apply just to teenagers; it is for every daughter who finds it challenging to be pure in an impure culture.

It's not the rules that change our hearts. We answer to a higher order. We answer to love. It is about a relationship with our heavenly Father. Rather than limitations, morals, and a code of ethics chiseled in cold stone, we have living truths penned on our hearts. When we turn our faith into a list of "do's and don'ts," we lose that relationship with the One who wants the best for us.

Heavenly Father, let my purity come from my relationship with You. Regardless of my past, I name You my protector and invite You into the most intimate spaces of my life.

I Am Strong

BECAUSE I AM EMPOWERED BY A RELATIONSHIP WITH THE FATHER, RATHER THAN RULES.

9

A BRIDE

As a bridegroom rejoices over his bride, so will your God rejoice over you.
ISAIAH 62:5

I love it that God likens us to His bride. Recently, two of my sons got married. I watched from the front row as both of them cried when they saw their brides approaching, which of course made me cry. The brides were radiant in white and perfectly adorned. I'd like to think that is how Jesus sees us. In Revelation 19:7 we read, "And his bride has made herself ready."

How do we do this? To explore the answer, let's delve a bit deeper. How does a bride prepare herself for her bridegroom? It is more than a beautiful dress, hair, and makeup; it is a preparation that takes place in the heart. Below are some of my thoughts:

- A bride longs to please her bridegroom in every way.
- A bride desires to be pure and passionate in all she does.
- A bride longs to be understood at a depth her words fail to communicate.
- A bride needs to feel safe when she makes herself vulnerable.
- A bride loves the freedom to express herself without fear.
- A bride delights in surprises and unexpected gifts.
- A bride loves to share secrets with her bridegroom.
- A bride loves to be chased by her beloved and to chase him in return.

- A bride loves knowing the joy of belonging.
- A bride desires to be nurtured, protected, directed, and even gently corrected.
- A bride is consumed with love for her husband.

I believe these desires and more are embedded in the heart of every daughter of God. We can dare to allow these wishes to stir our hearts because His deepest desire is to love us into all that He created us to be. Jesus, our bridegroom pleads, "Let Me love you."

No one else can love us this way. These longings run so deep that no earthly man can satisfy them all. Earthly love may escape and disappoint us, because we long for another. Your heavenly Prince will never disappoint or hurt you. He forged your deepest desires and has always been what your heart longs for.

He has provided all that you need. Why not wrap yourself in His righteousness? Adorn yourself with His adoration. Revel in His embrace, and let your heart dance before Him.

Dear heavenly Father, love me into all that You created me to be. Like a bride, I will prepare myself for You. Set me like a seal on Your heart, and as I walk into all You have for me, let me sense You smile.

I Am Strong

BECAUSE MY BRIDEGROOM REJOICES OVER ME.

Strong in Truth

WISE WITH WORDS

Gracious words are a honeycomb, sweet to
the soul and healing to the bones.

PROVERBS 16:24

The apostle John wrote to his friend Gaius, "Dear friend, I pray that you may enjoy good health and that all may go well with you, even as your soul is getting along well" (3 John 1:2).

John must have known that our health is affected by the well-being of our soul. There is no possible way to separate the two. They are intimately intertwined. Though words may not inflict physical harm, the Bible compares them to a lethal weapon and a healing balm: "There is one who speaks rashly like the thrusts of a sword, but the tongue of the wise brings healing" (Proverbs 12:18 NASB).

Hurtful and angry words act on us like painful stab wounds. One jabs at our shoulder, another grazes our stomach, and one finds its mark in the upper arm, and then our assailant runs away. We are stunned by the assault, and blood stains our clothes. Feeling faint we close our eyes for a moment, wondering how words could do so much damage.

Then we hear another voice. It is soft and gentle. We feel its warmth as a golden mist of light overtakes the darkness. Words of life and healing cancel out the very words that wounded us. *I love you. I am with you. You are mine.* Their gentle warmth calms the fiery pain. Each pleasant word acting as a restorative.

This is the power of words on our souls. Words can wound and words can heal. With this knowledge, let's use our words to free and heal others rather than stab and wound them. Rather than being careless with our words, let's be careful and choose to be wise with our words. By controlling what we say, we respect the power of words.

Simple words of encouragement and compassion could make all the difference for someone. We have within our power life-giving medicine when we speak from the Word of God. He alone is the healer so it is no surprise that His words carry healing. It costs so little to encourage others and benefits them in more ways than we may ever know.

The choice is yours. Will you speak harm or health today?

God, teach me the power of words and help me
use my words to bring healing and encouragement
to those You've put in my path.

I Am Strong

WHEN I CHOOSE TO USE MY WORDS TO BRING HEALING, WISDOM, AND LIFE.

2

UNDIVIDED

Teach me your way, LORD, that I may rely on your faithfulness;
give me an undivided heart, that I may fear your name.

PSALM 86:11

Many years ago when John and I visited Israel, I still remember what our tour guide told us about the Romans. He claimed they were somewhat benevolent conquerors, and even allowed the Jewish people to maintain their own religious beliefs, as long as they took on the Roman culture. They wanted them to look, live, and act like Romans. Invasion tactics haven't changed much since then.

The counsel of this present calls to us, "You may have your religion, as long as you endorse our system of belief as well. Don't be foolish—there is not one truth; there are many. You can believe whatever you want if you act like us!"

But, of course, this won't work for us. God never called us to be one with our culture. We are one in Him. This means we believe Jesus when He says, "I am the way and the truth and the life. No one comes to the Father except through me" (John 14:6).

We follow our Lord rather than whatever truth is the current trend. His Truth inspires us to leave behind our ways and rise to God's perspective. God's way of thinking is totally different than the way we process things. Empty words of compromise encourage us to remain the same by making excuses for our behavior. This world is not our home; we are just passing through, which means we no longer conform to our culture but are being transformed by our relationship with our Holy God.

We find our counsel in the Word of God rather than in the wit and wisdom of this present, jaded world. As Christ-followers we are called to encourage one another. This means we add courage to each other by speaking the promises of God. The world tells us, "Do whatever you want. You do you." But we are ambassadors of heaven walking the face of the earth in a time of great confusion. And rather than live for ourselves, we live for Him.

The Word of the Lord should not be watered down until it blends seamlessly with the wisdom of this age. The Word of God has always stood alone. We struggle when we walk with a foot in both worlds, because our affections are divided. In today's verse, David highlights our need for an undivided heart. I believe you are reading this because you desire to serve God with your whole heart. He wants there to be no struggle for our affections. He invites us to place our hearts in the safety of His care and then wage war on the enemies of our souls.

Lord, Your kingdom is my culture. Give me an undivided heart, that I may fear Your name.

— *I Am Strong* —

WHEN MY HEART IS UNDIVIDED.

3

WALLS

---

*In that day this song will be sung in the land of Judah: "We have
a strong city; He sets up walls and ramparts for security."*
ISAIAH 26:1 NASB

In ancient times, walls were erected around cities as a source of protection.
They were an obstacle that kept wild animals and enemies at bay. It is an
unfamiliar concept for us, but these cities were surrounded on all sides by
unscalable walls. They stood as a warning to those on the outside: "You will
not be allowed in until we know you are safe." They also served as a barrier
of protection for those who lived within the walls. The inhabitants of the
cities learned to trust the walls and the gatekeepers for their protection from
invaders and vandalism. These walls protected the citizens from the ravages
of sickness. The walls acted as barriers against wind, rain, and desert storms.

Now in light of this, imagine a city without walls, one that has been
invaded and looted at will. Enemies and invaders come and go as they
please. Who would want to live where there is no protection . . . where
there is no shelter?

When we do not protect our spirit, we inhabit a similar place. Our
heart is no longer a haven or refuge of safety and peace, but it becomes a
violated, looted city. We become subject to our moods, impulses, and any
lies or destructive words that pass through our ears. Frustration becomes
our daily bread, and sorrow and regret are our portion.

So how do we rebuild the walls that protect us? We can begin by adding intention to our words, by being mindful to use words that heal and build. Learn the Word of God and how it applies to your marriage, your work, your children, and your friendships. Bless these areas of your life and refuse to curse them. Allow the Word of God to transform your soul, and you will reap the benefits.

It is imperative that you allow God to disengage you from any entanglement or entrapment that occurred as a result of past outbursts or injurious words. These could be words you've spoken or the destructive words of others that were launched as missiles at your walls. Be mindful of the barrage of self-destructive words we use against ourselves, words like, "No one really cares about me. In the end I will be alone and betrayed." Or "I'm ugly and fat. Why would anyone like me?" These words wound us and cause our walls to crumble. Instead, search the Word for building materials—use God's promises to discover and declare the truth about yourself, and let them become a strong wall of protection around your heart.

Dear heavenly Father, show me the truth about myself and my life in Your Word. Help me build strong walls of truth around my heart, so I can flourish in their protection.

I Am Strong

WHEN I PROTECT MY HEART
WITH GOD'S WORD.

4

WALKING AROUND IT

"There is nothing hidden that will not be disclosed, and nothing concealed that will not be known or brought out into the open."
LUKE 8:17

When I moved to Colorado, I went shopping for a sofa for my family room. I remember finding one I really liked. I thought, "Here is the perfect sofa." It looked great backed up against the wall of the furniture store, surrounded by beautiful accessories and paintings. But then I remembered my sofa would not have a wall behind it. The sofa would need to look good standing on its own, without a wall to lean on. When I pulled the sofa away from the wall to look, I realized it wasn't going to work after all. If I had only looked at the front of the sofa, I would have taken it home. I would have loved it . . . until I caught a glimpse of its backside.

Most of us only see the upside of sin. We like the way it looks, the way it feels, and we say to ourselves, "I'll take it!" Only later do we check our backsides and experience the embarrassment.

But when we say or do sinful things in secret, it is not God who embarrasses us; we embarrass ourselves. It is like planting seeds in secret and becoming angry with God when a plant appears. Perhaps we believe we are capable of hiding things well enough that today's verse doesn't really apply to our circumstances. But if the Scripture says that nothing will stay hidden, it means it without exception.

Given this insight, it is important that we live with a greater awareness of our behavior. The book of Ephesians calls it living circumspectly. "But all things that are exposed are made manifest by the light, for whatever makes manifest is light. . . . See then that you walk circumspectly, not as fools but as wise" (Ephesians 5:13, 15 NKJV).

To live circumspectly means to live with the realization that the whole of our lives is connected and the time will come when an event from our past will catch up to us in our future. The root of the word *circum* means "to go around" or "to encircle." To "spec" means "to see or to look at something" much like a builder "specs" a home so potential customers may examine his skill before they purchase it. Likewise, we are charged to live our lives weighing out decisions and actions from every angle and point of view. We need to take a walk around our decisions, visit every room, and be certain we like the way it looks from every angle. Then we can act wisely and make good decisions that bring us strength.

Lord, remind me that to You everything is out in the open. There is nothing I can hide from You. Let me be circumspect in all my dealings, acting in ways that bring honor to You.

I Am Strong

BECAUSE I DO NOT LIVE ONLY FOR TODAY.

5

LEAVING THE LAND OF REGRET

Now there were four men who were lepers at the
entrance to the gate. And they said to one another,
"Why are we sitting here until we die?"

There comes a time when each of us must decide enough is enough. Regret eats away the human heart just as surely as leprosy eats away at human flesh. Strong girls know when it is time to get up and walk. To avoid a life of regret, live your life on purpose, with an eye to the future. We all need to walk with destiny in mind. Without a destination, a walk becomes a wander. There really is no other way of traveling to where you want to go. Perhaps you find yourself now in a place you did not wish to go. Maybe you're living in the gloomy land of regret. I have a secret to tell you: Regret will keep you in this place.

It is time for you to exchange the phrase, "If only!" for the phrase, "Even now." Regret will continue to echo in our lives until it is addressed head-on.

I believe each generation has the opportunity and mandate to redeem their mistakes by speaking the truth and warning the next generation, which is something we can never do if we wallow in regret. As we redeem our regrets we pass on a legacy of learning. This means the next generation will have the opportunity to stand higher, see clearer, and avoid the very pitfalls we fell into. This is not the time to sit listlessly in the regret of our past failure or to wander about without direction. It's time to walk forward.

God, I refuse to remain in the famine of my regrets. I am going to stand up and move forward so that others will find strength from my actions. I am exchanging my "if onlys" for "even now!" and embracing Your vision for my future rather than the regrets of my past.

I Am Strong

BECAUSE I REDEEM MY REGRET WITH PURPOSE.

6

A WOMAN
BELOVED

"For your Maker is your husband—the LORD Almighty is his name—the Holy One of Israel is your Redeemer; he is called the God of all the earth. The LORD will call you back as if you were a wife deserted and distressed in spirit . . ." says your God.
ISAIAH 54:5–6

Today's passage holds a special promise for women. God could have said, "Your Maker is your father," but He did not. He positioned Himself as a loving husband restoring a wayward wife. He describes the surety of His promise: "Though the mountains be shaken and the hills be removed, yet my unfailing love for you will not be shaken nor my covenant of peace be removed" (v. 10). No matter how intense the shaking in your life, God's love for you will never waver. Let this issue be settled once and forever in your mind.

This Scripture has no disclaimer! It includes women who are single, divorced, barren, or widowed. It encircles women who feel broken, less-than, inadequate, or too far gone. This promise spans all age groups. It is the voice of God speaking to His beloved and precious ones. He speaks peace to His women. So receive His peace and let it still any anger, anxiety, or fear in your heart.

Women are granted a unique opportunity. Everything about us is created to serve and nurture. But often we live in the fear of displeasing our heavenly Father, and we become weary in well-doing. We fear that no effort will ever be good enough, no sacrifice ever great enough. Remember, it is not based on what you do but on what was done for you. None of us could ever live a life pleasing enough to satisfy God's statutes. We must be women after His heart, but we will not pursue Him if we fear rejection and His wrath. This creates an atmosphere rife with frustration. God wants to release His daughters from this heavy burden.

You are a woman by His divine design and purpose. It is something to be celebrated because you are fearfully and wonderfully made—and unshakably loved.

Lord God, impress upon my spirit what manner of woman you would have me to be. I accept Your unwavering love and everything You have done for me. Bring me closer to You, to a place of peace in my womanhood.

I Am Strong

BECAUSE I AM DIVINELY DESIGNED.

7

NOT A SECOND-
CLASS CITIZEN

*"I will be a Father to you, and you will be my sons
and daughters, says the Lord Almighty."*

2 CORINTHIANS 6:18

When I became a Christian and realized that God actually loved me, it was too much for me to comprehend. In response to such beautiful mercy, I abandoned myself to His care. I never even thought of my femininity as an issue.

Then I went to churches and conferences where I heard things that clouded the issue of His love for me. Somehow I was getting the impression I had slipped into redemption as a second-class citizen of the kingdom. Now mind you, I don't believe anyone ever said it straight-out, but it was an undercurrent nonetheless: Women were not to be trusted and were barely redeemed.

My first confusing encounter happened while I was still in college. At a Christian conference, after a wonderful time of worship, the pastor opened in prayer and called his wife up to the platform. I watched as a gracious and lovely woman ascended a platform encircled by thousands. Then he began a series of jokes and put-downs, all of which she was the brunt of. She answered a few back in jest. The congregation laughed, but I felt a bit sick. His cuts seemed to dig a little deeper than hers did. It was as though she knew her limits, and he had none.

"Do you know where we men would be without women?" he asked genially. I hoped he was now going to say something nice after all the put-downs.

"Men would still be in the Garden." The whole place erupted in laughter. Was I the only one confused by the comment? Had I come out of one world of shame to be made fun of in another? My face went hot, and I felt tears trying to escape my eyes.

The next day, instead of joining the service, I made excuses and volunteered in the nursery. I was more comfortable believing God loved me as I rocked crying infants. As I held them, I imagined this was how God felt about me. Inside I was crying and He was speaking gently to me. I was His daughter; He was my Father. There was so much I didn't understand, but His love was certain.

Why do women accept it when cutting remarks are leveled against their gender? Is it because they are afraid? No, I am afraid it goes even deeper. They believe it is true on some level and, therefore, they deserve the abuse. But we do not. Don't believe it. God is not angry at women for being women. He did not create us as second-class citizens. He loves us as a Father loves a child, and His love for us is certain.

Lord, thank You for making me a woman. Show me the truth of my worth, and the truth of Your love. Embolden and empower Your daughters today.

I Am Strong

BECAUSE I AM HIS DAUGHTER. I AM NOT A SECOND THOUGHT; I AM HIS FIRST LOVE.

8

ALL YOUR LOVE

God is not a man, that he should lie.

NUMBERS 23:19 KJV

So many women live under the mistaken idea that their destiny is on hold until they have wed and been promised the undying love from the man of their dreams. Somewhere along the line we have forgotten that we are His dream. We don't have to wait for love to find us: it already has. Jesus first loved us. The question of whether we are loved or not should be settled.

Even so, for centuries, the daughters of Eve have cried out to the sons of Adam, "Give me all your love. Protect me. Meet my deepest needs for security and safety." When the sons of Adam answer, they make declarations they cannot keep in the hope that the daughters of Eve will meet the yearning they cannot verbalize. Both pursuits are doomed to fail because only God can meet those deep desires in each of us.

In John Eldredge's excellent book *Wild at Heart*, he shares the disappointment men experience when they look for their fulfillment from what he calls "the fair-haired maiden." Ah, but what of the women? Is not our hope just as displaced? We have looked for far too long at Adam for fulfillment, even though he was doomed to let us down. Adam was so much more than a husband to Eve. In some ways he was a type of father, for she was the only woman born of man. She was deceived into sinning by the serpent and then disappointed by Adam's choice, just as she was disappointed in her own. In truth, we want men who draw their strength from something bigger than us.

It is not the fault of the sons of Adam; they cannot give us the blessing we seek, and we frightened them by giving them so much power over our souls. We must learn the blessings we truly need come only from God. We must allow God to give us a new name, for we are no longer daughters of Eve, hiding in the shadows, but daughters of light and promise, His bride.

In our relationships with men we may find love, we may find companionship, we may find a life partner, but we will never find a Savior. Jesus alone is the Man who cannot lie, because He is the Truth. His Holy Spirit is nearer than the breath we draw. In Jesus we are rescued, protected, cherished, and made whole in ways that are only possible for the One who loves perfectly.

Lord, You are the Truth that cannot lie. You alone can make me whole. Forgive me for giving anyone but You that much power over my soul.

I Am Strong

WHEN I FIND MY COMPLETION IN GOD RATHER THAN MEN.

9

WALKING IN
THE LIGHT

But if we walk in the light, as he is in the light, we have fellowship with one another, and the blood of Jesus, his Son, purifies us from all sin.

1 JOHN 1:7

What does it mean to "walk in the light, as he is in the light"? To answer we need to look at a preceding verse, 1 John 1:5: "God is light; in him there is no darkness at all." God not only walks in light; He is Light. This light does not emanate from any external covering but proceeds from His very being. There is no darkness in any part of Him. This is a hard concept for us to even imagine let alone envision. Everything we see is shaded and shadowed in one manner or another. Every light source we know of causes shadows. The apostle John was not referring to a light source that originates or shines outside or around us but to one that proceeds from us.

John was not referring to natural, physical light but to the light of our spirit (though in heaven, as with Moses, it may actually be physically visible). We walk in the light in this present dark and shadowed world by walking in purity of heart. We remove areas of darkness in our lives by allowing the blood of Jesus to cleanse us. This restores and maintains our fellowship with other believers and with God. But, "If we claim to be without sin, we deceive ourselves and the truth is not in us" (1 John 1:8).

If we have any sort of self-awareness, most of us would never claim to be without sin. But this can happen, without us realizing it. When we justify, blame, or make excuses for our behavior, we in essence claim to be faultless. It can be heard in our conversations: "I'm sorry. I know I should not have . . . but (insert excuse here)!" For most of us this line of reasoning is all too familiar. We have said some form of it since childhood. But this is not an apology; it is a way of placing blame. We are not truly sorry until we take responsibility for our actions.

"I'm sorry, but you made me mad!" This is a blame technique that says we had no choice in the matter. First John 1:8 tells us that when we follow a pattern of claiming to be without sin we deceive ourselves and "the truth is not in us." It is one thing to have knowledge of the truth and quite another to live it.

God wants clean hands and a pure heart. These come through humility, transparency, and honesty.

Dear Lord, show me how to walk in
the light and stop blaming and making
excuses for any patterns of darkness.

I Am Strong

BECAUSE THE SOURCE OF LIGHT HIMSELF LEADS ME ON A PATH OF TRUTH.

Strong in
Relationships

NEVER REJECTED

His anger lasts only a moment, but his favor lasts a lifetime.
PSALM 30:5

What do you do when you know you've hurt or upset someone? I've learned the hard way that if I pull away, avoid that person, or make excuses, the relationship crumbles. On the other hand, if I turn my heart towards them, reach out—and here's the hard part—humbly ask for forgiveness, there is a chance for the relationship to heal. This is always the right approach in our relationships even if we don't see the right response from others. There are times when people will choose not to forgive you, but you must know this: God never will. His love and forgiveness always prevail. Even when it feels as though He has turned His face away, He will never reject you.

There are times when I know God is less than pleased by my behavior. The very moment I am honest with myself, repent, and ask for His forgiveness my heart is filled with His light and love. Even when I know I deserve judgment, He bathes me in mercy. He quickly assures me: "You are Mine. I love you. I believe you want to change. I have already forgiven you. Now it is time to forget it." In this moment He wants you to know the very same thing.

You are His child. He may reject your actions, words, or behavior, but He will never reject you. When you know you've done something that displeases your Father, turn towards Him rather than away. Pulling away or hiding lengthens the process and cheats us out of experiencing His "favor [that] lasts a lifetime." Open your heart and receive both His love and the lesson that is to be learned.

Father, I know You love me too much not to show me when I am in the wrong. Show me through Your Word and Your Spirit any area of my life that needs to be cleansed by Your mercy. I choose to run toward You, never away.

I Am Strong
BECAUSE I KNOW WHERE TO TURN WHEN I AM WRONG.

2

PEACE IN CONFLICT

*If it is possible, as far as it depends on
you, live at peace with everyone.*

ROMANS 12:18

*S*ometimes resolving conflict is easier said than done. When the
conflict is between Christians, we at least have the same frame of ref-
erence or standard for resolving issues. But sometimes people refuse to be
reconciled. Then what do we do? I have lived long enough to have had this
happen a few times. I'd inadvertently offended a friend and sensed there
was a breach between us. I searched my heart and went to her. I asked if
there was anything I had done to hurt or offend her. I volunteered the fact
that I realized that I could be offensive without my knowledge and assured
her I did not want to stay that way. She told me I had done nothing, yet the
measured distance remained. I bought her a gift and left a note, and again
asked for forgiveness. I received no response. I went again in person. She
assured me that no, there was nothing wrong, but still she still remained
distant. Finally I went to a mutual friend and asked her if she knew what I
had done to offend this person. She did not. I poured out the whole story
to her in an attempt to make sense of it. Finally, after listening to the whole
thing, she said, "Lisa, have you asked her to forgive you?"

"Yes," I assured her.

"Have you reached out?"

"Yes, repeatedly," I said.

"If you've done all this and she still won't receive you, you have to let it go."

Her words set me free. I realized that I had obeyed Romans 12:18: "If it is possible, as far as it depends on you, live at peace with everyone." I felt so guilty and at a loss because I wasn't even sure what my transgression was. The truth is, it is altogether possible that she no longer enjoyed our friendship, or the seasons in our lives had changed. I have watched some friends float in and out of my life as God has done a work in me or in them.

Our responsibility is to pray for reconciliation and ask God what role we are to play in the process. If we go to the person we wish to be reconciled with in humility and love and are still rejected, sometimes it is because they are not yet ready to respond. It might hurt, but you are never a failure if you obey God's Word.

Dear God, please give me the strength to be a reconciler in my relationships and the wisdom to know when others' reactions are outside of my control. As far as it depends on me, help me to bring peace.

I Am Strong

BECAUSE I LIVE AT PEACE WITH OTHERS AND WITH GOD.

3

AFFECTIONS AND DIRECTION

Keep me safe, my God, for in you I take refuge. I say to the LORD, "You are my Lord; apart from you I have no good thing." . . . I keep my eyes always on the LORD. With him at my right hand, I will not be shaken. Therefore my heart is glad and my tongue rejoices; my body also will rest secure.

PSALM 16:1–2, 8–9

Your affections will direct your decisions. Your affections will ultimately influence every area of your life. For those of us seeking to make God the center of our affections, the question becomes, "How do I set my heart on a God I cannot see?"

If you want to know how to do something, you talk with someone who has already learned to do it well. King David knew how to pursue God and maintain a passion for Him. He pressed into God like no other man before him. David never doubted God's love or faithfulness and lived his life in constant response and thanksgiving to Him.

In today's verse David is setting the Lord before him by bringing forth the declarations of his heart by way of his words. Our hearts are always revealed by the words we speak, whether in prayer, conflict, or conversation. Conversely, the heart is transformed by the words we speak as well. In this psalm, David brings out some powerful truths here that we need to make our own:

1. Make God your refuge . . . even kings cannot protect themselves.
2. Make it personal . . . call Him your Lord.
3. Tell Him there is nothing you desire more than Him.
4. Set Him permanently before you.
5. Give Him preeminence, and honor Him with your life.
6. Follow Him in everything you do.
7. Stand for Him because He's in charge.
8. Relax and rejoice since you're no longer in charge.
9. Rest in Him because of these powerful truths.

As we speak declarations of love and covenant with God, the bonds between us are strengthened. We enter into and have the ability to expand every relationship in our lives through our words and our corresponding actions. Words can heal and cleanse the sacred spaces of our lives just as they can wound our innermost beings.

To train your heart on God, choose your words the way you choose your friends . . . wisely. They may be few but precious. Pursue Him with the words of your mouth, and like David, you'll find your passion for Him growing.

*Dear Lord, I want to know You to pursue You as passionately
and intentionally as I would the most treasured human relationship.
As I open my mouth in prayer, let my affection for You grow.*

I Am Strong

**BECAUSE MY WORDS ARE SATURATED
WITH THE LOVE OF ALMIGHTY GOD.**

4

SAFE AND SECURE

The LORD is a refuge for the oppressed, a stronghold in times of trouble.
PSALM 9:9

*S*exual abuse and physical abuse are on an epidemic level. How would my Father want me treated?

This is a very important question to ask when it comes to relationships with the people who have intimate access to us. These people can range from a doctor or teacher to family and friends. It could be someone as close as a boyfriend or as intimate as a husband. But please hear me: If you are being abused or compromised in any way, it is not loving or healthy for you to remain silent. Do not stay in a relationship with those who abuse or misuse. Just as healthy, godly fathers protect their daughters, your safety is very important to your heavenly Father.

Your heavenly Father would never want you violated. He wants you protected and nourished. Don't be intimidated by other people or even your own poor choices. He will be there to back you up as you take your stand. Don't ever imagine He would make comments like, "You asked for it by being there," or "You've brought this on yourself." He would never say those things! He would say, "Get out, get home, and be safe!" You have every right to use your voice to expose abuse to the proper authorities.

This applies in romantic relationships, friendships, business associations, or with anyone you have close ties to. Luke does tell us to "pray for those who mistreat you," but prayer is just as powerful from a distance (Luke 6:28). Paul tells us, "If it is possible, as far as it depends on you, live at peace with everyone" (Romans 12:18). The phrase "as far as it depends on you" implies that, to some extent, it depends on them. You have both the right and the ability to take a stand and maintain a healthy distance from those who mean you harm. If you are involved with someone who is controlling, and you find that you cannot stand up to them face-to-face, then refuse to meet with them in person. And most certainly, you never have to put up with sexual or physical abuse—under any circumstance.

Creating space between you and someone who has harmed you not only protects you—it lets them know that their behavior is unacceptable and needs to be dealt with. You can forgive someone without giving them future access to you or your life. Forgiving them will protect the health of your soul that God values so highly.

You are a beloved daughter of God. Know how He would want you to be treated.

Jesus, give me Your strength and wisdom to handle any toxic relationships in my life. I trust You to stand with me.

I Am Strong

WHEN I SET LIMITS ON ABUSIVE OR HARMFUL RELATIONSHIPS.

5

WISE IN FRIENDSHIP

Better is open rebuke than hidden love. Wounds from a
friend can be trusted, but an enemy multiplies kisses.

PROVERBS 27:5-6

riendship can have a powerful effect on us. True friends will speak the truth to us, delivering words that may wound our pride but ultimately heal us. Friends who can be trusted will tell us what we need to hear rather than what we want to hear. On the other hand, we are warned that "bad company corrupts good character" (1 Corinthians 15:33). It is wise to surround yourself with people you want to become like, rather than with people you don't.

Here are some thoughts on how strong women choose friends:

First, make sure your friends are for you—not against you. Do you most often connect on a level of complaining? Do you leave their company feeling worn out, depleted, or angry? Strive to find friends who are invested in your growth—and be that kind of friend yourself.

Second, you want a friend who challenges you to grow and helps you focus on who you want to be. "As iron sharpens iron, so one person sharpens another," Scripture tells us in Proverbs 27:17. You want to have and be a friend who will speak the truth in love instead of flattering, coddling, or telling them what they want to hear. Disagreement can be healthy, and "wounds from [this kind of] friend can be trusted."

Be patient. Trust takes time. Friendship takes time. Intimacy is not the same thing as oversharing. You don't truly know someone just because you know more than you should about them or they know more than they should about you. I have seen friendships that spring up instantly and fade just as quickly. Like anything of value, healthy friendships require work. I have learned that I don't know if I have a real or fake friend until we have navigated a conflict.

Social media is not really set up to build friendships; it builds acquaintances. So be careful and intentional when choosing your friends. Pray and ask your Father for the right kind of friends for this season of life. He can reveal the difference between a "frenemy," and someone who is headed in the direction you want to go. If there is someone who consistently belittles, betrays, or leaves you out, ask yourself why you are friends. Check your motives. Are you stuck in an unhealthy pattern? Is it because you want to be popular? Pray to discern God's will through the Holy Spirit.

We can be kind, friendly, and on good terms with any number and all sorts of people. But for those you bring close and invest in, make sure that you both will speak truth in love with one another.

God, I know it is Your will for me to be in community and to grow in and through friendship. Help me choose wisely with whom to spend my time.

I Am Strong

WHEN I BEFRIEND THOSE WHO ARE GROWING WITH ME.

6

THE GOD OF JUSTICE

The one who states his case first seems right, until
the other comes and examines him.

PROVERBS 18:17 ESV

*A*nytime there is more than one person in a room, in a conversation, or on social media, there is potential for conflict. Too often those on each side of the argument will dig their heels in and refuse to listen because they believe they are the ones who are right.

When the children of Israel were under Egyptian bondage, they'd seen conflict resolved by violence and intimidation. In their new season of freedom they needed a healthy model of conflict resolution.

They had exchanged their lives of slavery in the land of Egypt for a life under the cloud and protection of God's presence. This meant moving from the rule of stone idols and blind images to a living God who is holy and righteous, loving and fearful. This God of fire and love was nothing like the Egyptian gods who were appeased with offerings. The Holy One of Israel was to be served in spirit and truth. And the very reason for His rule was justice. "But the LORD sits enthroned forever; he has established his throne for justice" (Psalm 9:7 ESV).

When we have been treated unfairly we can trust that in the end justice will be served. Woven deep within each of us is a desperate longing for justice, but if we are honest we have misjudged. There have been so many people or circumstances I was sure I was right about until I heard the other side of the story. This is the very reason for Paul's admonishment in 1 Corinthians 4:5 (KJV): "Therefore judge nothing before the time, until the Lord come, who both will bring to light the hidden things of darkness, and will make manifest the counsels of the hearts: and then shall every man have praise of God."

We can seek His wisdom in our conflicts and be relieved that ultimately it is up to Him to judge—and to save. Walking in His leadership, we can respond in righteousness and in mercy without having the responsibility to mete out punishment, take vengeance, or force compliance. We can pray to Him and watch Him act and give counsel. He is, after all, a Counselor who is always with us.

Lord, thank You that the pressure is off; I can trust You and defer to Your leadership in times of conflict.

I Am Strong
WHEN I TRUST THE GOD OF JUSTICE WITH CONFLICT.

7

GOSSIP-PROOF

Whoever derides their neighbor has no sense, but the one
who has understanding holds their tongue. A gossip betrays
a confidence, but a trustworthy person keeps a secret.

PROVERBS 11:12–13

We've all had it happen: You're having a nice conversation when someone in the mix starts gossiping. You look around the group in the hope that someone will put an end to it. But the longer you listen, the more uncomfortable you become with confronting it. You convince yourself that you can handle what you're hearing; after all, you're mature and wise . . . You'll be able to remain unbiased. What you won't realize until later is that your vision has been clouded. The next time you see the person who was discussed, it will be awkward. Or the next time you simply hear her name, you will feel the pressure to judge her, not just her actions but her motives. It's a challenge to avoid gossiping ourselves, but even listening to gossip taints us (Proverbs 17:4). This is a very real daily dynamic we must navigate in social media.

It will serve us well to first understand what a gossip does if we are to avoid being party to it. Merriam-Webster defines a gossip as "a person who habitually reveals personal or sensational facts about others." A gossip is in the habit of sharing intimate information with people who are not immediately involved in the situation. Everyone has gossiped at some point in time.

But someone who is a gossip does it without even thinking. Experience has taught me that their motive can be as innocent as wanting to feel valid and important or as dark as wanting to destroy someone's reputation.

Gossip poisons relationships and distorts the truth. Gossip is always a betrayal of trust. A secret, an incident, a conflict that could have been covered is repeated for someone else's gain. One person is sold out so the other person can gain security, position, or influence. People gossip to gain status, get attention, entertain, or make themselves feel better. Others gossip to punish or put someone in their place by judging them with their words.

That's not our place. The Holy Spirit tenderizes our heart so that if we talk about someone, we feel checked. If the enemy knows you are guarding what you say, he may try to trip you up with what you watch, read, or hear. Don't let him. Guarding against gossip is such an important part of guarding your heart. As you commit to pull away from these types of conversations, lean into the Spirit for wisdom on how to navigate these situations. Sometimes it is best just to get up and walk away. You don't want your mouth to take you down that dark path. Don't allow anyone to speak badly of those close to you. Instead, pray, love, and, when necessary, confront them.

Lord, place a watch over my mouth and ears so I don't taint my heart. Teach me how to gently but firmly hold my ground, edit my life, and respond to the check in my spirit.

I Am Strong

WHEN I SPEAK WORDS OF LIFE INSTEAD OF ANY FORM OF GOSSIP.

8

LIVING IN
HARMONY

Live in harmony with one another. Do not be proud, but be willing to associate with people of low position. Do not be conceited. Do not repay anyone evil for evil. Be careful to do what is right in the eyes of everyone.

ROMANS 12:16–17

To live in harmony or at peace with one another is to live in a way that is compatible, in tune, and in friendship with others in the body of Christ. This charge to live in harmony applies both inside and outside church walls. It is easy to lay aside any distinction we may think we possess, because in Christ we are all one. When we understand this, we will find friendship with unexpected people in God's service—no matter where their season of life places them. Today's verse warns us that pride and self-conceit will cause us to live in disharmony with others. One reason is that conceit will makes us think we have the right to repay evil for evil, which is the opposite of what Scripture encourages us to do. Remember, in Christ we are to embrace the nature of a servant. This means we live as examples of what is right by doing right.

When arrogance and pride are laid aside, we will turn the other cheek when slapped, give our coat when our shirt is demanded, and go the second mile. We are exhorted to go to great lengths to do right for the sake of others and, as far as it concerns us, to live in peace with everyone. This means developing a childlike trust of our Father. He alone knows all sides—every line on every page of the story. He is the faithful and true author.

We live in a time when the tension is so high and yet people still respond to kindness. As I move through my day, I look for people to notice. I compliment them, help them, or simply greet them. Far too many people are moving quickly through life with headphones on and eyes averted. I dare you to be strong and take a chance on kindness. Denying the existence of racial tension or financial pride does nothing to heal it. Let's be proactive. Pray that any and every area of prejudice that may be hidden in your heart would be exposed. If you find any, address it and repent. Lay aside any blinders of pride that would encourage you to justify it or make excuses and take up the mantle of humility.

Father, expose every area of pride and prejudice in my life
so I can live in peace and harmony with others.

I Am Strong

WHEN I LIVE IN HARMONY WITH OTHERS.

9

GROWING IN GODLY COMMUNITY

"You are my friends if you do what I command."

JOHN 15:14

*F*riends of Christ will be true friends to you. They'll speak well because they live well. "You are my friends if you do what I command" (John 15:14). Jesus is clear here. Friends keep His commands and encourage others to do the same. They don't keep the commands to prove their love for Him, but because they love Him.

True friends will always lift you higher and challenge you to walk in a manner pleasing to our Lord. They will want to spend time with you and will care about your growth. They will laugh and cry with you. Seasons of life may separate you, but because you are friends of the heart, when you get back together it is as if no time was lost. True friends will not be afraid of your growth, favor, or accomplishments but will celebrate with you as though they were their own. We all need a tribe of women behind, beside, and in front of us. These principles are just as true when you are young as when you are old.

"Though one may be overpowered, two can defend themselves. A cord of three strands is not quickly broken" (Ecclesiastes 4:12). Friends battle with and for you in prayer, interceding and lending strength you might not have on your own. Something powerful happens when friends gather in His name. Jesus said, "Where two or three gather in my name, there am I with them" (Matthew 18:20). This is an incredible blessing for this indispensable kind of friendship.

Friends search the Scriptures together and are amazed by the power of the Holy Spirit in each other. Be encouraged. God is doing a beautiful, deep work in His daughters here on earth.

There will be times when friends disagree, but that doesn't mean we should disband. Protect and cover one another because we were created to grow in community. Growth always means that there will be mistakes and mishaps, but when we are committed to one another, we expect the best rather than look for the worst.

If you don't have these types of relationships in your life, be intentional to build them going forward. Pray and ask for God's guidance and new ways to grow a godly bond. It may seem scary at first because some people don't want that level of commitment. Take a risk and extend your hand. Whether it's to join together in prayer, in study, or in enjoying each other's company, time with these ladies is something you simply cannot do without.

Jesus, I want to be a real friend and have real friendships. Show me where and how to build.

I Am Strong
WHEN I STAND WITH MY SISTERS IN CHRIST.

Strong in
Battle

WATCHFUL AND ON GUARD

*Be alert and of sober mind. Your enemy
the devil prowls around like a roaring
lion looking for someone to devour.*

1 PETER 5:8

Our enemy is on the prowl, hoping to catch us drowsy and unaware. Another translation uses the words *sober* and *vigilant* (KJV). The opposite of sober is drunk. Drunks are unaware of what is really happening around them. Their perceptions and perspectives are blurred, which slows their response time and distorts their reasoning. To be vigilant and alert is to be watchful and on guard, awake and attentive.

The verse in First Peter compares the devil to a roaring lion looking for easy prey to devour. He does not literally consume us; he devours us in other, more subtle ways. Though they are less obvious, they are no less dangerous. He devours our joy, peace, rest, strength, as well as attacking our health, relationships, and thoughts. He roars accusations to create a din of confusion. I believe God used the terrifying imagery of a hungry lion to illustrate the determination and persistence of Satan's pursuit. He easily catches the scent of offense and bitterness as surely as a lion detects its prey.

Lions are attracted to blood, and that comes from our wounded places. We must not let our wounds continue to bleed by ignoring the pain and covering them superficially. Part of being alert and vigilant means that we bring our wounds to our Father for healing. He will bind them up and heal us through the power of His Holy Spirit. Let's be vigilant even with the wounds that appear small and nonthreatening. When we catch them early, we can maintain our perspective and reasoning for the night's watch.

Father, keep me wise to the prowling activity of the enemy. Help me diligently bring my wounds to You, so You can heal them. Protect me, heal me, and teach me to be both self-controlled and alert as I fight on.

I Am Strong
WHEN I AM VIGILANT, TENDING TO ANYTHING AMISS.

2

PEACE BETWEEN THE SEXES

"I will put enmity between you and the woman,
and between your offspring and hers; he will crush
your head, and you will strike his heel."

GENESIS 3:15

*E*verywhere we look, it seems, we see a battle between men and women. Emasculated, angry men and wounded, angry women blame each other for their pain, and each wants the other to make it right. But neither men nor women can heal these places . . . Only God can restore us again to the garden of our dreams.

Ever since the serpent targeted Eve in the garden, the prophesied battle between the woman and the serpent still rages (Genesis 3:15). Daughters of God, earthly sons of Adam cannot save you from this serpent . . . It will take a heavenly Prince. The serpent's goal has always been the same: to strip the daughters of Eve of their dignity, strength, and honor and in so doing to render them powerless. And when women are stripped of their dignity and degraded, the men are shamed as well, for the woman is the glory of the man (1 Corinthians 11:7).

I want you to have the courage to see this struggle for what it really is: You are being stripped of your power, dignity, and clothing by a serpent!

You need to see this and be outraged. For only then will you be brave enough to fight your true enemy and give your total allegiance to the faithful and true King. Then you'll find garments to cover your nakedness with splendor. You will come to the realization that it is not men or our husbands we war against, but the enemy of our souls. We must awaken from the nightmare and begin to cry out for the restoration of the dream.

It is that cry deep in your soul of which I speak. You long for a deeper love, intimacy, and communion than a man can bring to you. You long for a safer haven than those found on earth. You cry out for the love of a heavenly Prince. And I have a secret to tell you, whether you believe it or not . . . He longs desperately for you as well. He is the very One who planted this seed of desire deep in the recesses of your heart, and He alone can fulfill your longings.

We will continually be frustrated in our search for fulfillment if we continue to look in all the wrong places. Men are not your problem, nor are they your answer! We need to lift our eyes heavenward, for our help comes from the Lord, the Maker of heaven and earth (Psalm 121:1–2). Only then and there will we find our source of joy and recover our strength and honor.

Father, when I'm tempted to battle the wrong enemies or look for fulfillment in the wrong places, remind me to look to You. You are my Redeemer, the source of my joy!

I Am Strong

WHEN I PROMOTE PEACE BETWEEN GOD'S SONS AND DAUGHTERS.

3

THE BATTLE OF UNFORGIVENESS

"A certain king . . . wanted to settle accounts with his servants. And when he had begun to settle accounts, one was brought to him who owed him ten thousand talents. But as he was not able to pay, his master commanded that he be sold, with his wife and children and all that he had, and that payment be made. The servant therefore fell down before him, saying, 'Master, have patience with me, and I will pay you all.' Then the master of that servant was moved with compassion, released him, and forgave him the debt."

MATTHEW 18:23–27 NKJV

Forgiveness is an act of healing. It frees us from bitterness and releases us from guilt. But forgiveness is also a key element in spiritual warfare. Your real battle is not with the one who hurt you but with the eternal enemy of your soul. When we forgive, we strip him of one of his weapons, because those who live in unforgiveness are susceptible to attack.

Today's passage grants us further insight into the dark recesses of unforgiveness. Put yourself in the servant's shoes. Imagine the terror of being brought before the King to settle a debt you cannot pay. Utterly helpless and hopeless, you prostrate yourself and beg him to have patience, that somehow and at some time you will pay it all back. But instead of agreeing to your terms, the King has mercy. Knowing you could never pay him back, he wipes out the entire debt. Your unbearable burden has been released! You are overwhelmed by the King's goodness.

Rather than follow the King's example of mercy, you remember that there are those who owe you. So you find them and demand they pay their debt—though they are just as hopeless to pay as you once were (Matthew 18:28–31). In the parable in Matthew, the forgiven servant does just this, and when the King finds out, he declares, "You wicked servant! I forgave you all that debt because you begged me. Should you not also have had compassion on your fellow servant, just as I had pity on you?" (Matthew 18:32–33 NKJV).

In the parable the King is our heavenly Father, we are the servant, our Christian brothers and sisters are the fellow servants—and the enemy of our souls is happy to play the role of the torturer. When we don't forgive, we imprison others in the chains of guilt and condemnation and are in turn turned over to the torturers to pay what we know we never can. I believe this describes a sort of hell on earth. We all have met people tormented by the very things they refused to forgive in others. When we behave in this way, we end up doing the enemy's work for him. It's time to remove the chains from one another.

Lord, reveal anyone I have imprisoned with my unforgiveness.
I choose to release them just as You have released me.

I Am Strong

WHEN I FORGIVE AS I HAVE BEEN FORGIVEN BY THE KING.

4

YOUR REFUGE

*"He will command his angels concerning
you to guard you carefully."*

LUKE 4:10

I often forget I have angelic protection, but I shouldn't. I love the imagery that David gives us in the Psalms: "Be merciful to me, O God, be merciful to me! For my soul trusts in You; and in the shadow of Your wings I will make my refuge, until these calamities have passed by" (Psalm 57:1 NKJV).

God is our protection. I learned long ago that my ability to protect myself was very limited. God is the One we should run to. Put down your phone when you've been falsely accused, slandered, or just plain lied about; close your laptop and run to the refuge of His wings. I do this by closing myself in a room, turning on music, and worshipping. Worship is always a great response when you don't know what to do. When you are overwhelmed with life, whatever the circumstances, you can find a shelter waiting for you in His presence.

Do not allow the enemy to trap you into defending or attempting to protect yourself; you will fall short. God invites us to hide ourselves in Him until the storm has passed and we can see clearly.

All lesser refuges are outside the shadow of His wings. Revenge and rage are never refuges, though they will lie and say they are. These false shelters must be laid aside in order to enter into God's presence. Defensiveness and self-reliance are a weak shelter indeed compared to Him. Escaping, self-medicating, or avoiding are only temporary means of reprieve, and all the counsel, self-help, or "proven solutions" in all the world cannot hold a candle to Him.

So when you feel calamities are about to sweep you under and you feel ambushed on every side, get excited. God is about to show up and do what you cannot. Not only does God instruct His angels concerning you, He makes Himself available as well. When the enemy rages, we have this assurance in Deuteronomy 3:22: "You shall not fear them, for it is the LORD your God who fights for you" (ESV).

When the battle is too big for you, draw near to Him.

Lord, You are my protection. I will draw near
and worship, trusting that You will fight
on my behalf when I am overwhelmed.

I Am Strong

**BECAUSE I AM SAFE AND PROTECTED
IN THE SHADOW OF GOD'S WINGS.**

5

WE ARE IN A BATTLE

For our struggle is not against flesh and blood, but against the rulers, against the authorities, against the powers of this dark world and against the spiritual forces of evil in the heavenly realms.

EPHESIANS 6:12

The enemy tries to trick us into thinking that we wrestle with the people we see, rather than with the unseen forces of darkness. Paul doesn't tell us this to frighten us, but to make us aware of what is really going on. There is an entire realm of darkness that we could never fight in our own strength. Paul continues, "Therefore put on the full armor of God, so that when the day of evil comes, you may be able to stand your ground, and after you have done everything, to stand" (Ephesians 6:13).

God has already provided everything we need to stand. The fact that Paul repeats this charge to armor up makes me think he does not want us to become casual with our weapons. He doesn't want us to imagine that we can go out half-dressed and unarmed and still have the strength to stand. What does it mean to stand your ground? It is to adopt a posture of determination that refuses to back down. Paul continues, "Stand firm then, with the belt of truth buckled around your waist, with the breastplate of righteousness in place, and with your feet fitted with the readiness that comes from the gospel of peace" (Ephesians 6:14–15).

We stand with our core wrapped in truth, our heart and vital organs hidden behind Christ's righteousness, and our feet ready with a gospel of peace. We live in a world desperate for peace. Truth and righteousness are precursors to peace. Compromising truth causes us to lose ground and be less than who we are. We are strong when we fight from a place of peace. In Christ, peace becomes a way to calm storms, heal hearts, and restore souls.

Heavenly Father, teach me how to fight from that place of peace in You. As I read Your Word, bind truth to my soul so that I will not compromise.

I Am Strong
WHEN I STAND IN TRUTH, RIGHTEOUSNESS, AND PEACE.

6

SHIELDS AND ARROWS

In addition to all this, take up the shield of faith, with which you can extinguish all the flaming arrows of the evil one.

EPHESIANS 6:16

We have been given a shield that shelters us from every flaming arrow that the evil one aims at us. Paul calls it a shield of faith. Hebrews 11:1 tells us, "Now faith is confidence in what we hope for and assurance about what we do not see." We certainly cannot see this faith shielding us, but we can develop it. Faith comes by hearing and studying the Word of God. I imagine faith as a force field. The more our faith grows the more we are shielded. Faith may begin with what we receive, but it should always grow into what we can give.

"Take the helmet of salvation and the sword of the Spirit, which is the word of God" (Ephesians 6:17). Salvation is the helmet that covers our mind. So many times when I was newly saved, a terrible thought would assault my mind. I would recoil in horror, wondering where it had come from. After I was saved I began to recognize the thoughts that were not mine. Salvation brings peace to our minds, and when a troubling or tormenting thought attacks we take up our sword! The Word of God is our sword of the Spirit. Like Jesus did when He was tempted by the devil, we speak what is written to the enemy of our souls. When he attacks our peace, we lash back with God's promise in Isaiah 26:3, "You will keep in perfect peace those whose minds are steadfast, because they trust in you."

Heavenly Father, thank You for the gift of
faith that shields me from the onslaught of
the enemy and for peace in my mind and
the sword of Your Spirit in my hand.

I Am Strong

AS I GROW IN FAITH BY READING, SPEAKING, AND LIVING THE WORD.

7

THE REAL WAR

For though we live in the world, we do
not wage war as the world does.

2 CORINTHIANS 10:3

We live on the earth, but we cannot war according to its ways. The question is not if we will fight but how we will wage war. This difference is best captured in our motive or our "why" behind the fight. We should always fight *for* rather than merely against. We also know a truth that runs far deeper than those who wage war according to this world: People are never our true enemy. I know there are times when this truth feels like a lie. Each of us can provide the names of those who have hurt us. But God loves all people. They are the ones Jesus came to save, so we should never fight against them. We war to free the captives rather than fight the captives. We attack the stronghold that holds them rather than the prison. Here is the reason: "The weapons we fight with are not the weapons of the world. On the contrary, they have divine power to demolish strongholds" (2 Corinthians 10:4).

We have been entrusted with divinely empowered weapons that are contrary to the weapons of this realm. Because they are more powerful we must be all the more careful. Never forget that our very words can bless or curse, so how much more will our actions? The weapons of this realm kill while our weapons give life. Worldly weapons divide people, nations, and cultures while our weapons of prayer unite us under His kingdom rule. The weapons of this earth are meant to wound and maim those we see as opponents, while our double-edged swords separate truth from lies so healing and restoration can begin. The weapons of this world were created by men to intimidate and paralyze others with fear, while our armament was forged in heaven to release and strengthen the fearful captive with courage so he is free to walk in the purpose of his divine calling. We attack the stronghold to free the captive.

Heavenly Father, whenever I find myself in a battle, show me what I am really fighting for. Holy Spirit, always remind me that I am to strike the stronghold rather than wound the captive.

I Am Strong
WHEN I WAR TO FREE OTHERS.

8

BATTLING IN
THE LIGHT

God is light; in him there is no darkness at all.

1 JOHN 1:5

In the book of Joshua, we read the story of a ferocious battle between God's people and their enemies. The Lord was battling right alongside them. Joshua, their leader, must have decided at some point that they needed more light to continue, so he said, "Sun, stand still over Gibeon, and you, moon, over the Valley of Aijalon." The Bible tells us, "So the sun stood still, and the moon stopped, till the nation avenged itself on its enemies. . . . The sun stopped in the middle of the sky and delayed going down about a full day. . . . Surely the LORD was fighting for Israel!" (Joshua 10:12–14).

Apparently the missing element in this battle was light, and God provided it in a miraculous way. In the sunlight they could see clearly their allies and their enemies. But in the dark it is easy to mistake an enemy for a friend and break rank. In the same way, in our spiritual battle, we need light to fight! And God offers us that light in abundance. He is the sun in our sky, dispelling the darkness that confuses, confounds, and saps us of energy. While our enemy thrives in the darkness, we thrive and have victory in the light of God's love and truth. "See, darkness covers the earth and thick darkness is over the peoples, but the LORD rises upon you and his glory appears over you" (Isaiah 60:2). Just as with the children of Israel, we are not controlled by the darkness that surrounds us because we have the rising of the Lord God's Son upon us. Israel's army must have thought it was impossible to stop the nightfall, but what is impossible with men is possible with God. Our God deals in the impossible. He answers, "I know you see darkness falling on the earth and on its people, but don't be afraid, for I am your covering of light."

As you battle, don't look at the darkness around you. Remember the light that is within you. God continues to shine down and dispel the shadows for you, even if it takes all day and all night.

Lord God, I am strengthened by Your light within me. Shine on me until the battle is done!

I Am Strong

WHEN I FIGHT BECAUSE GOD IS MY LIGHT.

9

DETERMINED

Take up your positions; stand firm and see the
deliverance the LORD will give you.

2 CHRONICLES 20:17

In this journey of life, you will want to quit. There comes a time in everyone's life when they just want to lie down and stop. What separates those who falter and fail from those who experience victory is their ability to get back up. There are so many battles that are won by simply outlasting the enemy. We will all get knocked down. You can't stop that, but it is up to you whether you get back up. Determine to persevere in faith—even when you don't feel strong. Your feelings will limit you because you don't actually know what you are capable of until you show yourself. As we stand firm, our Lord fights for us. It will be hard. When did we start imagining there could be a victory without a battle? Is there a battle that you keep drawing back from? Is there spiritual ground that you have backed off of? God is calling you back into position. He who promised you is faithful. God is strong and He wants you strong. He will reveal His strength to you so He can reveal His strength through you. When you are tired, when you want to stop, remember what He says in 2 Chronicles 20:17:

> You will not have to fight this battle. Take up your positions; stand firm and see the deliverance the LORD will give you, Judah and Jerusalem. Do

not be afraid; do not be discouraged. Go out to face them tomorrow, and the LORD will be with you.

The Lord fights for us. Sometimes the victory comes if we just keep showing up. We win as we keep loving, keep giving, keep serving, and keep learning. Other battles are won in song. When we sing the Word of God we are singing a sword of the Spirit. When we pray His promises we are singing a sword. Some battles are won in silence and surrender to Him. We are so confident that God is good and does good that we just smile confidently, knowing that He has it. When we go out in His strength, we can face anything that life throws at us—discouragement, exhaustion, or outright opposition. We are told, "Do not fear, for I am with you; do not be dismayed, for I am your God. I will strengthen you and help you; I will uphold you with my righteous right hand" (Isaiah 41:10).

Almighty God, I will stand in Your faithfulness as You fight for me. I choose determination and perseverance each and every day, until the battle is won.

I Am Strong

WHEN I STAND, CONFIDENT THAT THE LORD MY GOD IS FIGHTING FOR ME.

Strong in Grace

1

YOUR PAST IS NOT
YOUR FUTURE

---

*Jesus stood up again and said to the woman, "Where are your
accusers? Didn't even one of them condemn you?"*
   "No, Lord," she said.
   And Jesus said, "Neither do I. Go and sin no more."
JOHN 8:10–11 NLT

None of us is without sin, and too often we bed down with men,
religion, or the world for our affirmation. But these will always
disappoint us. Ultimately, sin and religion will betray you. In John 8, Jesus
gave dignity, power, and honor to a nameless woman who'd found herself a public spectacle. Jesus looked beyond the obvious and refused to
acknowledge her present state as her permanent condition. In essence He
told her, "Your past is not your future! Go, and sin no more! Sin was your
past, but godliness is your future. Bondage was your past, but freedom is
your future. Shame was your past, but dignity is your future. Nakedness
was your past, but garments of splendor are your future."

Jesus does so much more than forgive this woman . . . He sends her
away free. Forgiveness is where freedom begins. Freed from the bonds of
sin, grace moves us forward so that sin does not ensnare us again. First
Jesus lavishes us with mercy, then strengthens us by grace. "For sin shall

no longer be your master, because you are not under law, but under grace" (Romans 6:14).

Mercy deals with what we have done and grace empowers us to walk in a way that honors what Jesus did on our behalf. God's mercy and grace empower us to leave behind our sinful life and to step into His future and hope.

We have been given grace. The power of our former bondage has been broken. It's time to have more faith in the words of Christ, our liberator, than in the power of the chains. Their hold on you is not as great as His claim to you. Dare to believe, and leave behind the shadows of your past!

Heavenly Father, thank You for forgiving me and
gracing me with a future. I believe Your words
of light more than the lies of darkness.

I Am Strong
BECAUSE MY PAST IS NOT MY FUTURE.

2

FORGIVEN

Be kind and compassionate to one another, forgiving
each other, just as in Christ God forgave you.

EPHESIANS 4:32

had accumulated an overwhelming number of trespasses and offenses on my record when I finally became a Christian. When my husband, John, led me in a prayer of salvation, he had me repeat after him, "Lord, I confess my sins."

I panicked. "I don't know if I can remember them all!" I was afraid my salvation would be lost due to my faulty memory.

"You don't have to name each one; just confess you have sinned," John assured me. I was comforted because I was certain God had kept a much better record of them than I had. I knew I was a sinner, and I knew I needed mercy. I needed forgiveness, and I received it, by the grace of God.

But it wasn't far into my Christian walk before I found myself in a state of unforgiveness with other Christians, or should I say fellow servants. I felt they owed me something like an apology. I allowed this to eat at me. During this time I experienced a lot of spiritual warfare. I felt like a target—because I was. Even though I was a Christian I'd fallen prey to the schemes of the devil. I spent a lot of my time in prayer binding and loosing, but to no avail. I was bound by cords of my own making. When

I finally saw the truth, I realized it did not matter what was done to me. It didn't matter if I was right and they were wrong. All that mattered was obedience to the Lord's command to forgive as I had been forgiven.

I was overwhelmed by the extent of my own deception. I had thought I was so right when in fact I had been so wrong. With this realization, I freely forgave and cried out to the Lord to wash me anew in the cleansing river of His mercy, and of course He did. Let me just say, I've been bound and I've been free, and free is better. No matter how much humble pie you might have to eat, free is still better.

*Heavenly Father, reveal any deception and
areas of unforgiveness in my life.*

I Am Strong

BECAUSE I FORGIVE
MYSELF AND OTHERS.

3

GRACIOUS

The discretion of a man makes him slow to anger,
and his glory is to overlook a transgression.

PROVERBS 19:11 NKJV

The writer of Proverbs told us that it is our "glory" to overlook a transgression or an offense. It is to the honor, praise, eminence, and distinction of a Christian to overlook an offense. It is an example of our acting Christlike.

It is only possible to overlook insults, injuries, and threats if we have first committed ourselves to our Father, the righteous Judge. Often when my children were having a disagreement of sorts they would appeal to our sense of fairness. "He is not cleaning up enough" or "He has been on the computer too long." They wanted their cause heard and to hopefully get their way, and then to see justice served. John and I would step in and officiate as best we could, but frequently they thought our calls were not fair. This led to the disaster of them taking the matter into their own hands. I am not talking about conflict resolution; we encouraged that. It's payback. "Why did you hit your brother?" "Because he . . ." You've heard the list before. When we told them to bring the problem to us instead of hitting, we heard, "But last time you didn't do anything." Which translates to "I decided I didn't like the way you handled it; therefore, I'm not taking a chance this time. I will handle it!"

John and I are the first to admit that we made mistakes as parents, but the good news is that God does not! He is a righteous and perfect Judge. His decisions may not be in the timing or manner that we would suggest, but His ways are perfect while ours are flawed. When we overlook an offense, we are like trusting children who say, "Father, I know I can trust You with this one. It is too big and painful for me. I refuse to lash back; instead, I lay it at Your feet and forgive." It is a royal gesture. It is how we imitate the Son of God in our earthly lives. Jesus told His disciples, "If [your brother] sins against you seven times a day, and returns to you seven times, saying, 'I repent,' forgive him" (Luke 17:4 NASB).

There will be offenses that each of us will need to overlook. To overlook is to look above something; it is to choose to see things on a higher level than the offense was committed on. It is to extend grace and mercy when you'd rather exercise judgment.

Lord, make me gracious toward others, rather than hung up by offenses. May I reflect Your grace and mercy in all I do.

I Am Strong

WHEN I AM AS GRACIOUS TO OTHERS AS GOD HAS BEEN TO ME.

4

GROWTH, NOT GUILT

There is now no condemnation for those who are in Christ Jesus.

ROMANS 8:1

hy are we so hard on ourselves? What do we think it will accomplish? I used to go to bed each night and recite a mental list of each and every failing from the day. I would beat myself up with it, whipping myself with the shame of any remembered mistake in an attempt to pay a penance for my infractions. You might end the day disappointed and upset with yourself and imagine that by punishing yourself you will somehow emerge changed and different. But this is not true. This pattern is destructive rather than constructive.

It's not wrong to realize you have made mistakes or to wish you had done things differently. It is healthy to allow the Holy Spirit to bring to mind errant words and actions. But this reflection is for growth, not guilt. Each night I berated myself with the failures of the day until I felt smothered by their weight. Only then would I allow myself to pray and ask for forgiveness. But at that point guilt had me in such a stranglehold that I found it difficult to believe the next morning's mercy would be enough to cover it.

For example, if I was disappointed with the way I had handled my children during the day, I pressed the issue by attacking myself with questions like, "Why are you so impatient?"

Rather than look for ways I could be more patient, I labeled myself a failure, which only served to set me up to fail again.

Self-loathing and self-anger create a destructive pattern of guilt.

Jesus understood that the weight of guilt was too much for us to bear, so He bore it for us. Our faults should be brought to the light of His Word. There we find counsel and insight rather than accusation and guilt. What the light reveals, it also has the power to heal. Guilt is darkness; mercy is light. Rather than rehearsing our wrongs, let's rehearse the answers that make it right.

*Dear heavenly Father, forgive me for berating
and beating myself up. Let the light of Your Word
permeate my heart with truth. Help me turn from
my self-judgment and embrace Your mercy.*

I Am Strong
BECAUSE I CHOOSE GROWTH
RATHER THAN GUILT.

5

THE HEART GARDEN

Looking carefully lest anyone fall short of the grace of God; lest any root of bitterness springing up cause trouble, and by this many become defiled.

HEBREWS 12:15 NKJV

When I was a young girl I was often given the task of pulling weeds. I was always in a hurry to get the job done and over with so I could play. In my carelessness I would often snap off the top of the weed instead of pulling it up by the root. I had to pierce the dirt to grab hold of the base, and I didn't want to mess with that. Without the stem and leaves I thought the plant would die, and my mother would never know what was underground. I'd rake dirt over the gnarled stumps and run along. A few weeks later another weed would be in its place. It was smaller than the original one I had snapped off, but it now possessed an amazingly stubborn root system. My mother showed me how it would now be necessary for me to dig around the base of the plant and expose enough of the root to get a death grip on it. What began as an easy chore had now turned into a tedious battle.

How often do we do the same thing with the gardens of our hearts?

Satan longs to plant seeds of hopelessness, wrong thinking, or anger in us until the root of bitterness chokes the nourishing seedlings of the Word of God.

Weeds grow faster and easier than plants do. They are wild plants that travel freely, adapting to any type of soil they find. On the other hand, the life-giving seeds of fruits or vegetables must be cultivated carefully and are easily choked out by surrounding weeds or the wrong soil conditions.

Roots of bitterness will spring up at the most inopportune times, when they are the most inconvenient to be dealt with. Though they may be inconvenient, they should not be ignored because they will become deadly if left unaddressed. Don't be tricked into allowing them to remain unchecked, and never snap off the visible part thinking it will deter the root. It will not; it will only serve to strengthen it. Too often we are satisfied with the mere illusion that everything is under control, rather than allowing the Holy Spirit to do a deep work in us.

So let us be vigilant gardeners. If we detect bitterness in our hearts, (it tries to come up in every season) we can take it to the Master Gardener, who will help us expose the root system in order to destroy it. If His Word sinks deep into the soil of our hearts, we will cultivate a beautiful harvest.

Father, help me be diligent in cultivating my soul, never afraid to expose the roots of bitterness that may grow in me. Alert me to every small shoot, and empower me with Your strength to uproot what doesn't belong.

I Am Strong

WHEN I TEND TO MY HEART LIKE A GARDEN.

6

THE JUDGMENT BOX

"Do not judge, or you too will be judged. For in the same way you judge others, you will be judged, and with the measure you use, it will be measured to you."
MATTHEW 7:1-2

Most of us like things in neat boxes. We are more comfortable if we know what fits in each compartment. If we can't fit something or someone into our boxes, we often pass judgment. But that really says more about us than the person we are judging. I remember being tormented in my thoughts by a situation that occurred when I had been a Christian for a few short years. I just couldn't sort it into a neat box.

There was a Christian couple who openly testified how God had joined them in marriage. We'd spent time with both of them and knew they both genuinely loved God and His people. Suddenly there were all sorts of ugly rumors, and before you knew it they were in the throes of divorce. There had been no adultery; it just seemed they weren't compatible. This really threw me for a loop. I was struggling with issues in my marriage and was trusting God to work them out because I was certain He had brought John and me together. Yet, this couple, who had also said God had brought them together, had bailed.

This shook my confidence that God could do something in my marriage. I felt compelled to find some type of fault with this couple. If I could disqualify them, I could squeeze them into a box.

I took my inner turmoil to a trusted counselor, expecting a long, well-thought-out biblical answer. But instead he just sighed and said, "That's a tough one. I'm glad I don't have to judge it."

Immediately I felt the weight of the situation lift from me. His simple words had set me free from my burden. He was right. I had allowed Satan to stir my heart to judge others and it caused me to doubt the faithfulness of God. I had measured my marriage by theirs and limited God to what I thought He hadn't done for them. I had judged out of fear.

We often judge to safeguard ourselves from injury or criticism, but really each and every one of us is guilty. The verse after today's passage reads, "Why do you look at the speck of sawdust in your brother's eye and pay no attention to the plank in your own eye?" (v. 3).

Jesus reminds us that we need to remove the plank of judgment in order to see clearly and truly be of help to others and ourselves. When we can't fit others into our boxes, let's examine our own hearts—and be thankful that it is not our job to judge.

Father, when I judge others, remind me that the same measure of judgment I use on them will be used on me. Help me to sow mercy because I need mercy.

I Am Strong

BECAUSE I'M LIVING LIFE OUT
OF THE JUDGMENT BOX.

7

OWNING UP AND LETTING GO

If we confess our sins, he is faithful and just and will forgive
us our sins and purify us from all unrighteousness.

1 JOHN 1:9

There is so much freedom in this promise. When we confess our sins, He not only forgives, he purifies us from the aftermath of our choices. Why is it that we try to shift the blame by making excuses? I have learned that once you own a mistake it no longer owns you. There is no reason to play the blame game when Jesus took our blame; we confess and move on.

First, let's talk about owning up. When I was growing up there was a comedian named Flip Wilson who played a character named Geraldine, who always made the excuse, "The devil made me do it!" We can get creative with our excuses, but the truth is the devil can't make anyone do anything they don't want to do. I believe there is another way that we inadvertently shift blame and offer excuses. It is when we say, "I couldn't help it" or "I just couldn't control myself." It is when we contradict God, who says we can do all things through Christ who strengthens us, by saying sin has a hold on us and we are not able to master it. We may not say it with our mouths but more than likely we will say it with our lifestyles. Repentance says, "I did it, I repent of it, and I turn to You, Lord, to wash me clean."

After we own our mistakes there comes an even harder step: letting go. You must release yourself. This is crucial because it is a key factor to your emotional, physical, and spiritual health. No good comes from trying to punish yourself for something God has already forgiven and forgotten. If He has removed your iniquity as far as the east is from the west (Psalm 103:12), it is senseless for you to bring it up.

It is the goodness and kindness of God that lead us to repentance. This goes against everything ingrained in us. We want to pay; then we will feel released from our guilt. I grew up being told, "I will believe you are sorry when you change." But God extends His mercy when we don't deserve it so that we can change. Mercy is when we don't get what we deserve. This is a difficult concept for most of us to understand. We are more comfortable with rules and "an eye for an eye" and "a tooth for a tooth." The law, our enemy, and the accuser in our head will always ask for judgment while the Spirit grants mercy. Accept that mercy, friend. Accept God's path to freedom from sin.

Lord, reveal to me any ways I am resisting
Your provisions for freedom from sin. Show
me where I need to own up and let go.

I Am Strong

WHEN I OWN MY MISTAKES AND ACCEPT THE MERCY I DON'T DESERVE.

8

EQUIPPED TO LIVE IT OUT

---

*Whoever hates his brother is a murderer, and you know
that no murderer has eternal life abiding in him.*

1 JOHN 3:15 NKJV

There is far too much hatred in our world. It is time we took this verse to heart. Whoever hates his brother is a . . . what? Murder enters by the doorway of hate. First this Scripture opens up by addressing "whoever," and whoever includes every one. There is no exception clause that reads, "Anyone who has really been mistreated by their brother or brethren is excluded." When we read whoever, anyone, or everyone, it means the Scripture applies to each of us. We don't have an opt-out clause.

Now here is the good news: This is an opportunity for us to gain strength and grow in grace. As we submit to His Word, He will equip us to live out the truth. This verse says that whoever hates his brother is a murderer. There is no way around it—that is strong. I don't want to be called a murderer. Yet there have been times in my Christian walk when I found hatred hiding in the dark recesses of my heart. Does this mean I am eternally condemned as an outlaw or even a murderer? Not if I repent and refuse to allow the darkness to remain and grow unchecked.

We have experienced the empowering grace and the covering mercy of God. There is no sin too dark or heinous that He will not forgive it. God forgives murderers who repent.

We view life from a kingdom perspective, rather than from the perspective of our earthly judicial system. We are no longer mere citizens of this earth, for Scripture tells us, "You are no longer strangers and foreigners, but fellow citizens with the saints and members of the household of God" (Ephesians 2:19 NKJV).

We are governed by and answerable to the higher ways of heaven rather than the laws and courts of this earth. Heaven is not governed by outward rules and regulations etched in stone; it transforms us by the secret code written on our hearts. Dead, lifeless rules are for dead, hard hearts. The law of liberty is for hearts of flesh. This is why in the courts of earth you must actually kill to commit murder, but in the kingdom, merely hating sets us up as one. It is time we deal with any shadowed hatred in our hearts and confront a spirit of murder.

Heavenly Father, reveal any areas of hatred in my heart. I renounce it as I would the sin of murder. Forgive me even as I forgive them.

I Am Strong

WHEN I DEPEND ON THE SUPERNATURAL POWER, MERCY, AND GRACE OF GOD.

9

NO CONDEMNATION

"Then neither do I condemn you," Jesus declared.
"Go now and leave your life of sin."

JOHN 8:11

These are the words our Lord speaks to obviously guilty women.

Sadly, Satan's most vicious offensive against the daughters of Eve is often launched under the guise of religion. In John 8 we see clearly the cruelty of law and religion and the beauty of God's mercy and love. Let's visit this scene together and perhaps see it in a different light.

In the dim light of early morning, a large crowd waits to listen to a young rabbi named Jesus. Jesus is so different. When He speaks, you hear the words of the Father God.

At the first gleam of dawn, Jesus appears with His disciples. After greeting a few in the crowd, He sits down to teach. They listen closely, their hearts hanging on every word. But there is a disturbance on the horizon.

Over the heads of Jesus and His disciples, another group approaches. Their angry voices and dark forms are struggling with someone. It is the religious leaders, dragging a disheveled woman who clutches a remnant of cloth, attempting to hide her nakedness. It is obvious she was dragged from a bed of shame. The man, however, is nowhere in sight.

They say to Jesus, "Teacher, this woman was caught in the act of adultery. In the Law Moses commanded us to stone such women. Now what do you say?" (John 8:4–5).

What will Jesus say to such a woman? At first, He is not willing to look at her or to answer them. He bends down and writes in the dust.

Then He speaks only to the accusers, challenging the one without sin to throw the first stone. One by one they leave. They leave until it is only Jesus, the crowd, and the obviously guilty woman. Even though Jesus is sinless, He refused to throw a stone at this woman. He alone is the righteous judge, who had come to save rather than to condemn her.

Jesus is silent until all her accusers are gone.

Jesus straightens up and asks her, "Woman, where are they? Has no one condemned you?"

"No one, sir," she [says].

"Then neither do I condemn you," Jesus [declares]. "Go now and leave your life of sin" (John 8:10–11).

She lifts her head and meets His gaze. In His eyes she sees forgiveness, love, and even pain. She is no longer a daughter of death and darkness but of life and light.

When the serpent drags out our shame and accuses us, we can look to those very eyes, and know that He does not condemn us. His mercy defends us, and His Grace tells us we can "Go . . . and sin no more."

Lord, thank You for defending us when we could not defend ourselves. Thank You for saving rather than condemning us.

I Am Strong

WHEN I LET THE SAVIOR DEFEND ME BEFORE THE ACCUSER, AND THEN RISE OUT OF MY SHAME.

Strong in Self-Control

LISTENING CAREFULLY

Do not be quick with your mouth, do not be hasty in your heart to utter anything before God. God is in heaven and you are on earth, so let your words be few.

ECCLESIASTES 5:2

Scripture has a lot to say about the power of our words and governing our mouths. However, it is also important to pay attention to the power of listening. Listening requires discipline and takes time and patience. It means we ask the questions that will help us understand what is being said so we can go deeper. It is so important for people to feel heard.

This requires fighting the urge to assume what other people are thinking—they just might surprise us. I believe the quote goes, "Everyone you meet has something to teach you." We grow when we are constant learners. Don't listen so you can talk; listen so you can learn. Resist the urge to be formulating your response while the other person is still talking (like couples do in fights). There is something so honoring about truly hearing someone's heart. People know when you are not listening. I travel a lot and God gives me many opportunities to share His love and light on a flight; the conversation always starts with listening. People will hear what you have to say if you hear what they have to say. Listen to their needs, their hurts, and their thoughts. Then ask the Spirit to speak through you.

Listening well to others can awaken something within you as well. Let's not miss out on what we might learn because we are too quick to share what we already know.

Proverbs warns us, "Sin is not ended by multiplying words, but the prudent hold their tongues. The tongue of the righteous is choice silver, but the heart of the wicked is of little value" (10:19–20). Choice silver is refined by fire. When we allow the fire of God's Word to purify our conversation, impurities and indiscretions are removed from our conversations. The book of James encourages us to be slow to speak. There are so many times I have been saved by slowing down what I was about to say. The more I listen the slower I am to speak.

Even in conversation with God, we are encouraged to be of few words. He is in heaven while we are merely earthbound inhabitants. An integral part of the proper fear or respect of God is to know when to speak and when to listen. We learn by listening, not speaking. This means that your prayer life should include time for listening. There is no such thing as an awkward silence with God. Pause. Listen—to God, and to the people He puts in your path, and you will grow stronger.

Lord, help me to hear what people are really saying and respond as You lead. Train my heart to listen for Your voice each day.

I Am Strong
WHEN I LISTEN WELL TO
GOD AND TO OTHERS.

2

APPETITE CONTROL

"All things are lawful for me," but not all things are helpful. "All things are lawful for me," but I will not be dominated by anything.
1 CORINTHIANS 6:12 ESV

I'll admit it: I've developed an appetite for dark chocolate and coffee. I wonder if I would still occasionally crave good dark chocolate if I had never tasted it. And what about coffee? If I'd never stirred a heaping tablespoon of Breyer's coffee ice cream into my cup of java and sprinkled cinnamon on top in a desperate attempt to stay awake one morning, would I still crave mocha lattes?

Of course I wouldn't! And I wouldn't know what I was missing. I wouldn't have developed a taste for these delicious things. As long as I only knew coffee as a thick, black, bitter liquid, I despised it. As long as chocolate was only in the form of white or milk, I had no trouble resisting it.

Actually, there is no struggle! I do not fight my occasional urge for chocolate or my morning ritual of flavored coffee . . . I indulge them! They are not my masters but a part of a comfort ritual I go through. I can go a week or more without dark chocolate, and no one will be hurt. I will not be grumpy, but I do enjoy it when I have it. As far as the coffee, if I want to wake up suddenly instead of slowly emerging from a fog, I drink it.

But what if I allowed my enjoyment of them to override my desire for other healthy foods? What if I decided the sensual pleasure (provided by the dark chocolate) and the heightened state of awareness (supplied by the coffee) were more important than any other feelings in my life? Perhaps then mixed green salads would no longer have any appeal, because they wouldn't make me feel the same way chocolate did. Maybe all my other food and drink choices would seem boring and mundane.

What if I slipped away from reality and for two weeks existed solely on the merits of chocolate and coffee? I'd be happy, thin, and awake . . . at least for a while. Then everything would tilt out of balance, and my appetites would have to be brought back into check.

My point is, we develop our own appetites and desires. Whether it's for food, sex, entertainment, or social media, any appetite can become addictive enough to displace reality and throw us off balance. That's why we must be strong and self-controlled rather than controlled by our appetites. We have the power to increase or diminish their influences by the importance we assign them.

Heavenly Father, show me how to evaluate my appetites so they don't tip out of balance. Give me the wisdom to know how much is too much of anything in my life, so that I am not enslaved to anything.

I Am Strong

BECAUSE I GOVERN MY APPETITES
AND BUILD BALANCE RATHER
THAN LET THEM CONTROL ME.

3

IT'S OKAY TO
BE ANGRY

Be angry, and yet do not sin.

EPHESIANS 4:26 NASB

The first part of Ephesians 4:26 is easy enough: "Be angry." I can accomplish this without even trying. God tells us to be angry because it is okay to be upset. Anger is as valid a human emotion as joy, sorrow, faith, and fear. Even God gets angry—as a matter of fact, quite frequently. The Old Testament records several hundred references of His anger with Israel and other nations.

When an emotion is suppressed because it is not validated, it will eventually be expressed inappropriately. Conversely, if an emotion is expressed without restraint, then sin will follow upon its heels. God Himself validates human anger. Yet most of us do not even understand it. Is it throwing things and yelling and screaming at our loved ones? Is it holding a grudge over treacherous treatment? No, these are examples of inappropriate expressions of anger. There is a fine line between anger and sin.

The American Heritage Dictionary defines anger as "strong, usually temporary, displeasure without specifying manner of expression." It is okay to feel intense or strong displeasure over an event or at someone's actions—disapproval, dislike, or annoyance. These feelings are common to all of us and may be daily occurrences. It is the "and yet do not sin" part that takes some work. It would be wrong to expect the same reactions from a toddler as we would from an adult. As we mature, so should our ability to exercise self-control. It is not wrong to be upset, but it is wrong to punish other people because we are upset. As Christians we no longer only represent ourselves. We are His representatives, which means we must take a step back and consider how our reactions affect others. None of us can control what happens to us, but we are all in control of how we choose to respond.

Lord, please help me steward my emotions well, with the maturity and grace that is appropriate for a child of Yours. Show me the fine line between anger and sin, and guide me with Your spirit when I venture too close to it.

I Am Strong

BECAUSE I CHOOSE WHAT I DO WITH MY ANGER.

4

WATCHING
YOUR WORDS

*We all stumble in many ways. Anyone who
is never at fault in what they say is perfect,
able to keep their whole body in check.*

JAMES 3:2

The book of James goes on to illustrate the importance of taming your tongue in verses 3 and 4:

> When we put bits into the mouths of horses to make them obey us, we can turn the whole animal. Or take ships as an example. Although they are so large and are driven by strong winds, they are steered by a very small rudder wherever the pilot wants to go.

What we say can drive the direction of our life for good or for evil. Words not only direct us; they can be agents of destruction. James goes on to compare what we say to small sparks that can ignite a great fire. None of us wants to burn the place down! On the other hand, the book of Romans reveals the power of words to redeem and transport us from a kingdom of darkness to a kingdom of light. We are promised in Romans 10:9–10:

If you declare with your mouth, "Jesus is Lord," and believe in your heart that God raised him from the dead, you will be saved. For it is with your heart that you believe and are justified, and it is with your mouth that you profess your faith and are saved.

The very thing that gets us into trouble can get us out of it: "The tongue has the power of life and death, and those who love it will eat its fruit" (Proverbs 18:21). We are patterned after our heavenly Father, who uses His words to create and give life. This means we can choose to bless or curse with our words.

I believe this is an opportunity for constant learning. Let's speak in such a way that it leads to life rather than towards death and destruction. Your life will follow your mouth, so make sure you are saying where you want to go.

Dear Lord, watch over my mouth. May my words act like a rudder that takes me in the right direction, speaking words of truth and light rather than destruction.

I Am Strong
BECAUSE I GOVERN MY SPEECH.

5

REDEEMING REGRET

Godly sorrow brings repentance that leads to salvation and leaves no regret, but worldly sorrow brings death.

2 CORINTHIANS 7:10

We all experience regrets, but we shouldn't let them rule our lives. Destructive regret can lead to what Paul called "worldly sorrow." What is worldly sorrow? It is grieving about the loss of things, such as reputation, money, possessions, relationships, or other things that are attached to this world. This type of sorrow focuses on these losses without realizing the pain that our actions may have caused to others. This type of regret will try to bring about change on its own or through religious efforts. But this approach rarely goes to the root of the motive of the heart.

Godly sorrow moves beyond the concern for consequences and focuses on any damage that's been done in relationships with God or others. It is constructive rather than destructive. Godly sorrow helps us see things as they really are. David models godly sorrow in Psalm 51:1: "Have mercy on me, O God, according to your unfailing love; according to your great compassion blot out my transgressions."

David appeals to God's unfailing love and confesses that he has sinned against God. There is no line of defense in his words. There is no blame. He owns his mistake and openly acknowledges his sin. When we own our mistakes they no longer own us. We all need unrestrained mercy; as we humble ourselves, God will lift us out of our circumstances.

David knew he couldn't cleanse himself, so he turned to the Lord. God alone has the power to not only forgive our sin, but to banish every trace of shadow and stain.

David understood that sin dulls the heart and weakens our resolve. The psalm prayer progresses with: "Restore to me the joy of your salvation and grant me a willing spirit, to sustain me. Then I will teach transgressors your ways, so that sinners will turn back to you" (Psalm 51:12–13).

These verses are quite possibly my favorites in this psalm. They promise restored joy and a new beginning where there's been regret and sorrow. God can make something beautiful out of our ugliness. Then our failures become an opportunity to teach others about the faithful mercy and love of God. It is my prayer that our heavenly Father would transform every dark place of regret into shining beacons of His faithfulness and truth. In this way He triumphs in our redemption. I challenge you to turn every place of pain into a living example of beauty and freedom as you teach others about the love and truth that has set you free. This is the radiant result of godly sorrow.

Lord, may my sorrows be godly instead of worldly. When I experience regrets I will bring them to You in repentance and experience Your healing. Thank You for making beautiful things out of our messes.

I Am Strong
BECAUSE I TAKE MY TRANSGRESSIONS TO GOD.

6

ROOTED IN
THE WORD

"Keep this Book of the Law always on your lips; meditate on it day and night, so that you may be careful to do everything written in it. Then you will be prosperous and successful."
JOSHUA 1:8

Nothing strengthens us quite like the words of the Bible. That's why building a practice of retreating daily into God's Word is so important. As you read and apply the Word of God, you do not remain the same. Your heart softens and becomes tender to the things of your Father. This makes you more open to His leading. Studying Scripture is the spiritual discipline that brings life and energy to all other spiritual disciplines.

As with anything in the kingdom, it is not how many Scriptures you know but how many you live. This way the Word is made flesh in your life and produces fruit.

So where should you begin?

There are any number of places to start, and an endless variety of study plans available. Whether you choose a read-through-the-Bible plan, a written study on a topic that interests you, or a simple search for verses that speak to the issues of your life, make a point to spend a certain amount of time in the Word every day. Don't take on so much that you know you'll become burned out, but do make a point to open the Book every day. That time will soon become an anchor in your life.

With a pen and a journal, pray and ask the Holy Spirit to speak to you through Scripture. Reflect on the scriptures you've chosen, and then take it a step further—write in your journal how you will apply the truths you've learned. What is your action plan to integrate these truths into your life? What will you do in the next twenty-four hours or weeks to come to care for that seed of truth planted in your heart? Are there ways to track your progress?

When we think of discipline, we often think of something we don't want to do or even the idea of a punishment. But time in the Bible is like the discipline of eating healthy. It is a discipline that refreshes and enlivens even as it calms. It is a sacred space to seek out what God has to say to you, and to purposefully allow His words to revitalize every part of your life. Today, whether it's for five minutes or a whole afternoon, begin the healing practice of Scripture study and see how it strengthens you.

Father, thank You for providing me with Your words.
Build in me a thirst to find life in them each day.

I Am Strong

WHEN I PLANT GOD'S WORDS IN MY HEART AND WATER THEM WITH PRAYER, CARE, AND INTENTION.

7

SOWING AND REAPING

A man reaps what he sows. Whoever sows to please their flesh, from the flesh will reap destruction; whoever sows to please the Spirit, from the Spirit will reap eternal life.

GALATIANS 6:7–8

It's the law of sowing and reaping. When we plant the right things, we harvest the unimaginable. Scriptural seeds yield a strong and nourishing harvest.

Years ago, I planted scriptures in my heart in the hope that they would bring forth a harvest of righteousness. One of my favorites was found in the book of James: "My dear brothers and sisters, take note of this: Everyone should be quick to listen, slow to speak and slow to become angry" (1:19).

I was modeling the exact opposite of this behavior. I was quick to speak, slow to listen, and quick to wrath! I didn't have it right in a single area.

I enlisted God's help for my mouth. Like David prayed, my prayer became: "Set a guard over my mouth, LORD; keep watch over the door of my lips" (Psalm 141:3).

This guard is posted so the wrong words won't escape and do their damage. I have learned that the Holy Spirit will take the scriptures in your heart and bring them up at just the right time. This acts as a warning before the wrong words escape.

Science tells us it takes twenty-one days to break a habit. Habits are strong. They are the responses we have without thinking. There was a time when rage had become a habit in my life. To imagine twenty-one days without an infraction was impossible. It might as well have been twenty-one years. Rage was that ingrained in me.

Well, how do you break a habit? You break one the same way you developed it. One incident at a time, five minutes at a time, one hour at a time, one day at a time. This was the approach I adopted to break the cycle of rage. Before I even rolled out of bed I prayed, "God, I need You today. Place an extremely ruthless and severe guard over my mouth. I don't want to sin against You or anyone else. Help me to be slow to speak, quick to listen, and slow to wrath." These scriptural reminders became my daily prayer and strength.

I am not going to lie and tell you it was easy; it was not. But I can tell you that with God all things are possible. I have lived more than two decades now free from the control of rage. This was my wonderful harvest from planting and acting on two small seeds of scripture.

What will you plant in your heart today? What do you want to harvest? Search the Word for seeds, plant them, and God will give the increase.

God, show me the scriptures that I need to sow in my soul. I believe that as I sow and act on them in faith, You will give the harvest.

I Am Strong

BECAUSE I PLANT GOD'S WORD IN MY HEART AND ACT ON IT.

8

THE STRENGTH
OF REST

By the seventh day God had finished the work he had been
doing; so on the seventh day he rested from all his work.

GENESIS 2:2

When the issue of the Sabbath comes up, many of us feel a twinge of guilt. As women, we rarely feel a release from the ever-present needs that demand our attention. We are taunted by piles of laundry and constantly reminded of our to-do lists that are out of control. We have families that legitimately need us to be active. Even getting the entire family out the door to go to church is a labor. It's not that we want to ignore the fourth commandment ("Remember the Sabbath day by keeping it holy," Exodus 20:8); we just don't think we can afford to rest. Ultimately, it's an issue of trust. We are concerned that if we stop—if we rest—God won't be able to take care of us.

Really, the concept of a day of rest (Sabbath) is an invitation into health and restoration. More often than not Sunday is not a day of rest for me, so I have learned to capture a Sabbath in other ways. Even Jesus invited His disciples to take a break from ministry: "Come with me by yourselves to a quiet place and get some rest" (Mark 6:31). He knew that if they continued to run themselves ragged, they would be no good to anyone in ministry, and they would suffer. I've learned the hard way that when I am tired, I am not capable of making good decisions. When I feel overwhelmed I will say "no" to the very things I should say "yes" to and "yes" to the things I should say "no" to. Then living with those bad decisions further exhausts me.

Why not give yourself permission to accept His invitation to rest? Pick a day, a half-day, or even a few hours (it doesn't even have to be Sunday), and set it apart for the restoration of your body and soul. Be intentional, plan ahead, turn off your phone, close your laptop, and tell people ahead of time that you will be off-grid enjoying your life. This is a great time to laugh with your children, enjoy your friends, or capture time with your husband. Go out to eat or cook the day before. Stop rehearsing the to-do list. Shut the laundry-room door. Put aside any work you've brought home from your job. It will all get done, just not today. Enjoy your God-given day of rest. Use this span of time to protect, nourish, and guard your heart. Then you'll be refreshed for the work God has for you.

When you're at work, work—diligently and to the best of your ability—and in your time of rest, rest! Accept God's invitation to rest as a chance to reset.

Lord, I don't want to burn out. Show me how to balance work and rest in a way I should to take a real Sabbath rest.

I Am Strong

WHEN I REST, TRUSTING THAT GOD IS ULTIMATELY IN CONTROL.

9

AN AMBASSADOR
FOR GOD

You are a chosen people, a royal priesthood, a holy nation, God's
special possession, that you may declare the praises of him who
called you out of darkness into his wonderful light. Once you
were not a people, but now you are the people of God; once you
had not received mercy, but now you have received mercy.

1 PETER 2:9–10

In the Olympics, the winners are recognized and adorned with a medal, and the flag of their nation is draped over their shoulders to designate the country each participant represents. What would happen if, in the middle of the awards ceremony, a gold-medal gymnast from America decided she wanted to represent Canada? Would they let her? Of course not! She was chosen as an ambassador for America, not Canada; it is the American culture and people she is there to represent and inspire.

In many ways it is the same for us. We are representatives and ambassadors of heaven. We are here to leave an impression on those we meet that communicates whose we are and what kingdom we represent. The apostle Paul calls us "Christ's ambassadors" (2 Corinthians 5:20). And Peter calls God's people a "royal priesthood." We bear the honor of being both ambassadors and part of His royal family of priests. Why would we ever want to switch allegiances and represent a kingdom that isn't our Father's? Peter continues:

> Once you were not a people, but now you are the people of God; once you had not received mercy, but now you have received mercy. Dear friends, I urge you, as foreigners and exiles, to abstain from sinful desires, which wage war against your soul. Live such good lives among the pagans that, though they accuse you of doing wrong, they may see your good deeds and glorify God on the day he visits us. (1 Peter 2:10–12)

Once we were not God's, but now we are. Once we were under God's judgment; now we've experienced His mercy. In other words, once we were in this world and under its sentence of judgment, but now we are not of this world; we are of God's kingdom. This makes us aliens and strangers on this earth where we were once citizens. As priests, we are God's representatives and ambassadors on this earth.

Today, as you make your choices, as you act and react, remember on whose podium you stand. Live "such good lives" that others will glorify God and join us in lifting our voices in a mighty anthem of praise.

Lord, I am so proud to be an ambassador for You. Let my
life and my actions reflect Your goodness and grace.

I Am Strong

BECAUSE I REPRESENT A KINGDOM OF GLORY, A ROYAL PRIESTHOOD, CROWNED WITH GOD'S MERCY.

Strong in
Freedom

RELEASED
FROM SIN

Jesus replied, "Very truly I tell you, everyone who sins is a slave to sin. Now a slave has no permanent place in the family, but a son belongs to it forever. So if the Son sets you free, you will be free indeed."

JOHN 8:34-36

When the Son sets us free . . . we are "free indeed." What does this word "indeed" mean? It means without question, "truly and of a certainty." People may question your right to freedom. Your past might try to shame you back into the confines of your mistakes, but as far as God is concerned the sway of sin and shame in your life is over. People may want to still throw stones at you, but the words of Jesus echo release over the sin in your life. "'Then neither do I condemn you,' Jesus declared. 'Go now and leave your life of sin'" (John 8:11).

Once we confess, it's time to move forward and leave behind the sin, shame, accusations of others, and the guilty conscience of self. As we move from our darkness into His light we are empowered to go and sin no more. If God says you are not condemned, you are set free to walk in that truth. In this matter you cannot trust your feelings because they will lie to you. We will never feel righteous because in and of ourselves there is no righteousness. We are not the righteousness of God through our works or behavior but in Christ alone. This empowers us to move away from our past failures and mistakes and move forward. "Forget the former things; do not dwell on the past" (Isaiah 43:18).

Our today is no longer tied to our failures of yesterday. We are free to step into a new manner of life, cleansed by a mercy that is new every morning.

Heavenly Father, I embrace Your mercy. I will allow it to triumph over every area of judgment in my life. I leave this place of guilt and self-loathing. I rise and go to sin no more.

I Am Strong

BECAUSE THE ULTIMATE JUDGE HAS RELEASED ME FROM ALL GUILT AND SHAME.

2

A NEW HEART

*"I will give you a new heart and put a new
spirit in you; I will remove from you your heart
of stone and give you a heart of flesh."*

As Christians, we are constantly trying to keep a tender heart or, as the Bible calls it, "a heart of flesh." This is a heart that grows in compassion, love, and in sensitivity to God's leading. Heaven governs by a sacred code of love written on our heart. Dead, lifeless rules etched in stone are for dead, hard hearts. The law of liberty is for tender hearts of flesh rather than hard hearts of stone.

I should warn you, though, tender hearts have a greater capacity for both love and pain than stony hearts do. If allowed, hurt can harden our hearts, and if we are not careful it will slowly but surely displace the things of God in our life. Feeling heavy and drained is a symptom of this. A heavy heart finds it harder and harder to forgive others. It is exhausting to live on the edge of bitterness or resentment.

The good news is that even the hardest heart can be liberated by the truth of God's Word. I discovered hatred in my heart even after I became a Christian. I chose not to allow it to remain. Your heart requires guarding, to be sure it remains free from unresolved offenses—free from rage, hatred, envy, or other sins that so easily entangle us. One way we guard it is by continually exposing it to truth. It takes work, humility, and honesty. But your heart is worth the fight.

Even now there may be a reasoning war in your mind. One side brings up the names of those who have hurt you, imploring you to forgive and release them. The other side argues that you are justified in your hatred or resentment of them. Surrender to the first voice. Don't imagine that a hard heart will protect you . . . It won't.

Father, I confess any hardness of heart.
Break any outer shell with the rock of Your
Word so that a heart of flesh is revealed.

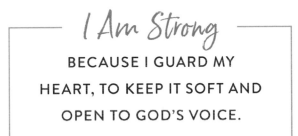

I Am Strong

BECAUSE I GUARD MY HEART, TO KEEP IT SOFT AND OPEN TO GOD'S VOICE.

3

THE POWER OF CONFESSION

Therefore confess your sins to each other and pray for each other so that you may be healed. The prayer of a righteous person is powerful and effective.

JAMES 5:16

Confession is one of the most difficult of the spiritual disciplines. Why is it necessary? We know we are forgiven as we confess our sins to the Father. But the book of James takes it a step further and tells us it is necessary to confess some sins to each other and pray with one another so we will be healed. I believe this is true for three reasons.

First, the kingdom does not operate on natural principles. Remember, Jesus told the Pharisees that whoever looks at a woman with lust has committed adultery with her in his heart. Heart issues are of the utmost importance in the kingdom. Our hearts are hotbeds for good or bad seeds. In the case of the Pharisees, the sin hadn't actually physically happened, but it had occurred in their hearts.

Second, by humbling ourselves through confessing our sin and praying with our fellow Christians, we position ourselves for healing. Healing flows into the dark recesses of our hearts when we bring sin into an open and safe environment. Confession sheds light on areas of sin and shame, and in this atmosphere of light, prayer begins the healing and restoration.

The third reason is that confession gives us a level of accountability. With confession comes responsibility. The Word tells us: "Faithful are the wounds of a friend" (Proverbs 27:6 NKJV). When I confess, I don't need sympathy; I need someone to wound me with the truth. And after praying together, I feel a load of shame lift off my shoulders.

But there remains the issue of habits. Jesus says in Matthew 16:24, "Whoever wants to be my disciple must deny themselves and take up their cross and follow me." Confession is another way of "taking up our cross," acknowledging our utter dependency on God. We "deny ourselves" the right to fix ourselves, or break cycles of sin on our own. Confession is a discipline that shows that we know we can't do it alone. But with God's help and the help of our family, we begin to heal.

Father, show me the healing that comes with confession. Lead me to the right people, and make me honest, brave, and open enough to take up my cross in this way. I want to follow You, and I acknowledge that I cannot do it on my own.

I Am Strong

WHEN I TAKE UP MY CROSS, MAINTAINING ACCOUNTABILITY AND RESPONSIBILITY.

4

FREED FROM SIN

We should live in this evil world with wisdom,
righteousness, and devotion to God, while we look
forward with hope to that wonderful day when the
glory of our great God and Savior, Jesus Christ, will
be revealed. He gave his life to free us from every kind
of sin, to cleanse us, and to make us his very own
people, totally committed to doing good deeds.

TITUS 2:12–14 NLT

This is great news! Sin no longer has any real power over us. It doesn't matter how many times we said yes to sin in the past; it has no place in our future. We have every right to turn from it and say no when sin tries to entice or entrap us with shame! Jesus broke its power, extended mercy to us, and empowered us to live by the grace of God. In Christ we don't receive the judgment we deserved because He took our sins upon Himself. We are forgiven and born anew out of death and into life. Beloved daughters, the enemy of your souls doesn't want you to know this. He wants you to remain in shame in the hope of entangling you again in sin. He doesn't want you to know you have dominion over sin, but it's true. Certainly in our own strength we will try and fail, but we are no longer alone in our battles. We are in Him, and our weapons are mighty!

Jesus, thank You for destroying the power
of sin. I reject the enemy's lies and turn
from them, toward You. Your death
gave me all I need to win this battle.

I Am Strong

BECAUSE CHRIST GIVES
ME POWER OVER SIN.

5

WHEN IT HURTS
TOO BAD

---

*He will wipe every tear from their eyes. There will be
no more death or mourning or crying or pain.*

REVELATION 21:4

I want to encourage you to release your pain. You may wonder, "How does one leave their pain behind?" You may challenge that I don't understand your pain or know what was done to you or how badly you hurt. And you'd be right. I don't know—but there is Someone who does. There are more wounds than can be listed. For certain I know some of you were molested or abused by someone you trusted. Some were raped or violated by a stranger. Maybe you were abandoned by someone who promised to always be there. Perhaps your child died a violent or senseless death. Someone you loved mistreated you. Your parents rejected you and you never felt good enough. Far too many were mocked for the color of their skin. Others were made fun of for a handicap. And sadly, most of us have been betrayed by a friend.

Any one of these tragedies and others I haven't listed are painful enough to wound us deeply. Then when we are in our most vulnerable state Satan seeds our wounded soul with words of bitterness and thoughts of revenge. He encourages us to rehearse the injury and to remember the pain. He wants us to press it tightly into our chest and never release it. He lies by promising that holding it in will protect us from future violations. But that is a lie.

There is healing in releasing your pain to Jesus, the only One who truly understands. The book of Isaiah tells us Jesus "was pierced for our transgressions, he was crushed for our iniquities; the punishment that brought us peace was on him, and by his wounds we are healed" (Isaiah 53:5).

Holding onto your pain will only further injure you. I want you to close your eyes and picture yourself giving Jesus all of the pain. He will not belittle what was done to you. Release it and allow Him to carry it away and redeem it.

Jesus, I believe You are my healing so I can trust You with every fragment of pain. I refuse to carry what I was not designed to hold. I release (name the areas of pain) into Your care. Redeem it for Your glory.

I Am Strong

BECAUSE I GIVE MY PAIN TO MY HEALER.

6

FIRM IN FREEDOM

It is for freedom that Christ has set us free. Stand firm, then, and do not let yourselves be burdened again by a yoke of slavery.

GALATIANS 5:1

Once we are free, it is a challenge to believe we are truly free—forever. Our culture and the bondage of religion will work their hardest to enslave us again. They want us to wear again the "yoke of slavery"— letting ourselves be dragged down by that heavy, nagging weight that ties us to shame and the sins that once enslaved us. Freedom happens both at once and over time. Jesus frees us when we give our lives to Him—and that freedom is ours to claim. Then, over time, we continually exercise this freedom by "standing firm" against the sin that once burdened us—by not accepting the yoke of trying to be perfect in our own strength.

So stand strong in your freedom! Stand against any guilt and shame that would try to lure you into a depression of defeat or back to a lifestyle of sin. Stand against every shadow of past shame that challenges your right to say no to fallen patterns. Perhaps in the past you had a hard time saying no because of guilt and shame—but you are freed from your past and your future is bright and free!

Because of the freedom and the glorious hope Christ gives us, we have no reason to fear our Lord and Savior's return, for He has redeemed us from wickedness and made us His own. Before, we were eager to do evil . . . Now we are eager to do good! When we are truly born again, our natural desires change. He forgives us and then changes our nature with the words, "Go and sin no more." It is not a prerequisite for forgiveness—forgiveness was already extended. It is a vote of confidence and a belief of better things to come.

The words of Jesus could be paraphrased this way: I do not condemn you. I forgive and release you from the sentence and judgment of sin. Now go, and sin no more. You are free! (John 8:11). We could never earn the mercy we're extended, just as we could never walk in godliness and say no to sin and worldly passion without the grace of God. Sin no longer has claim to our lives because: "It is for freedom that Christ has set us free."

Lord, I am so thankful that Your forgiveness and redemption are mine. Show me how to exercise my freedom by helping me turn away from the things that enslave.

I Am Strong

BECAUSE CHRIST HAS SET ME FREE.
THE EVIDENCE OF THIS FREEDOM
INCREASES IN MY LIFE EVERY DAY.

7

UNBOUND

We are not children of the bondwoman but of the free.
GALATIANS 4:31 NKJV

When I was a kid my father rarely connected with me—except to express his pride in how tough I was. His pet names for me were "tiger" and "little scrapper." Somehow dresses and feminine things didn't fit with these images. I was determined never to be a sissy or a girly girl.

Then one Saturday in junior high while watching a movie, I found the image of a woman I identified with. There was nothing frilly or lacy about her. Her life was an exciting adventure. She was one of the elite Bond girls (as in James). I was definitely more comfortable with the image of chicks wearing hot pants, packing guns, and running with the boys. Those girls held their own with the men, and no one dared push them around. They weren't going to wait for some man to protect them. They'd do it themselves.

But here's the thing about Bond girls. If I remember correctly, at least one of these women got killed in every 007 movie. In the end, James always bedded the remaining live one, but they were never seen together again. He went on to be part of the next adventure, but they were not. There was always another beauty to pursue once he was finished with them. I guess they truly were "bondwomen," enslaved to a system that did not know their worth.

I know this rough, tough, and sexually confident woman might at first look brave, but she isn't. All bondwomen are afraid at one level or another, especially if they're not in control. (Why do you think they pack guns?) Many of them never got the protection and love they needed from their fathers when they were little girls, so they decided to take matters into their own hands. Others were loved and nurtured, but they listened to a culture that encouraged them to trust in their ability to protect themselves instead of in God. But eventually all bondwomen find themselves on the outside looking in. Just because a woman is sexually desirable doesn't mean she is free.

Our culture gives us more opportunities to relate to the captive daughter than to the free woman. But we don't have to choose between these two "types," playing the flowery fainting female or the aggressive seductress. God made women with as many countless, brilliant options as there are daughters. Don't buy into the lie that you are limited to some man-made stereotype. We are His royal daughters, not bondwomen who have to trust in things that will ultimately let us down. And as His children we are free to be who we are, knowing we are fully and uniquely loved.

Father, I want to embrace everything You made me to be. When I am tempted to play a lesser role remind me of who I really am.

I Am Strong

BECAUSE I AM NOT BOUND TO A FICTITIOUS IMAGE OF MY WOMANHOOD—I AM A DAUGHTER OF THE LIVING GOD.

8

MADE NEW

If anyone is in Christ, he is a new creation; old things have passed away; behold, all things have become new.

2 CORINTHIANS 5:17 NKJV

When Christ becomes our Savior and Lord, the eternal penalty of our sin is removed as far from us as the east is from the west (Psalm 103:12). Sin no longer has mastery and legal grounds to hold your spirit in bondage. You are set free. Yet, freedom and forgiveness do not eradicate practical or natural consequences of sin. If I commit a crime and I am sentenced to jail and then get saved, my spirit is free but my body is still headed to jail. This doesn't mean I was not forgiven. It means I seek His wisdom as I deal with my realities.

You may wonder then how this truth applies: I am forgiven and have become a new creation. The old has passed away, and all things have become new for me. This truth is being worked out in us. We are forgiven and our sins are washed away the moment we confess them. We are made new spiritually in that instant when we experience the overwhelming mercy of Christ. But this does not mean my previous choices will no longer have any effect on me. I am no longer guilty and under eternal judgment, but some consequences remain.

For the sake of further argument, what if I had become pregnant during my wild, single days? It would have served as a wake-up call for sure. What if I became a Christian after becoming pregnant? Would the baby disappear? No, of course not! The presence of a child would not in any way negate my forgiveness of sin, just as the forgiveness of my sin would not erase the existence of the child. The baby is not a sin. She is the result of the choices I had made. The child would be loved and celebrated as a gift, even though the conception took place outside the covenant of marriage.

God is in the business of redeeming our mistakes, mishaps, and sin. Miracles don't always look like we expect them to, and beautiful things can be constructed from broken pieces. Nothing is impossible for God, but when the heart is broken, it becomes His first concern. He takes away the stony broken heart and replaces it with a heart of tender flesh. We can trust Him when He says we are being made new.

Lord, show me the difference between eternal forgiveness and natural consequences. I trust in Your ability to make me whole in every way that counts.

I Am Strong
WHEN I TRUST GOD'S ABILITY TO REDEEM MY REALITIES.

9

FREED TO BE HIS

"I am the LORD *your God, who brought you out of Egypt to*
give you the land of Canaan and to be your God."

LEVITICUS 25:38

How many of us have heard the question, "If you died tonight, do you know for certain where you would go?" The purpose of the question is to get the audience to ask themselves, "Do I know for sure I'd go to heaven?" If they don't, they have an opportunity to pray and assure their eternal positions. But eternity is more than an after-death destination; it is a way of life now. The following verse reveals God's deepest desire and purpose in liberating Israel from Egypt: "You yourselves have seen what I did to Egypt, and how I carried you on eagles' wings and brought you to myself" (Exodus 19:4).

I love the beauty and power of this verse. The mighty King of heaven swoops down to valiantly rescue His children after four hundred years of slavery. In the process, He strikes Egypt, the most powerful nation in the world, and reduces it to a humiliated wreck. The Israelite slaves receive the Egyptians' silver and gold.

This wasn't just His desire for Israel; it is His desire for you.

Our passionate and holy God is pursuing you! He is waiting and watching for you to glance His way. He longs for you to read the love notes He's woven throughout the scriptures in the hope that you will return His advances. He wants to release you from the captivity of a world trapped in darkness into life in His world of light. He longs to snatch you from the arms of faithless lovers and bring you into His faithful, everlasting arms. He wants to deliver you from the hard taskmasters and cruel bondages of this world in order to show you His tender love and mercy.

The rescue was never just about a promised land; it was about the One who made the promise. He ultimately wants to bring us to Himself. The promises in the Old Testament were merely a foreshadowing of things to come. God's ultimate purpose in salvation was to restore His children to Himself. Beloved, redemption is so much more than fire and life insurance!

Who doesn't long to be swept away from this world's cruelty and carried off to the mountain of God? After all, this world is not our home, so it is only right that we should nurture this longing. We should all welcome the escape from bondage and judgment, but salvation doesn't stop there. Let's lean into becoming His.

Father, thank You for freeing me so that nothing hinders me from being Yours. I choose to pursue the promise of knowing You.

I Am Strong
BECAUSE I WAS RESCUED TO BE HIS.

Strong in Holiness

NOT OF THIS WORLD

"You do not belong to the world, but I have chosen you out of the world."
JOHN 15:19

Jesus makes it clear that this world does not possess us. How should this reality work its way into our conduct? This world—and, more specifically, its culture—encourages us to conform to its behavior. But we no longer belong to our culture; we are in relationship with people and with God. We are called to be different than our culture, loving when it is hateful and kind when it is cruel. This difference also extends to our moral compass. The book of Ephesians gives us our true north: "But among you there must not be even a hint of sexual immorality, or of any kind of impurity, or of greed, because these are improper for God's holy people" (5:3).

There is no gray area in this verse. Why so stringent? I believe it is because even a hint can send mixed messages, which can be confusing to others. Because we are God's, we honor Him in all we say and do. This means the words we speak and our conduct should reflect His influence on our life. In Christ we are more than forgiven; we are holy. We are light where we were once darkness.

Ephesians continues, "Nor should there be obscenity, foolish talk or coarse joking, which are out of place, but rather thanksgiving" (5:4). Paul adds to the list confusing behavior, obscenities, foolishness, and coarse talk. Nothing of these conversation types is in keeping with godliness, and they only serve to muddy the water for those who are searching.

Instead of punctuating our conversation with obscenities, we are to be fluent in gratitude. In this way we maintain an attitude of thankfulness for God's favor and mercy. This alone should be enough to keep some of us talking for quite a while. Rather than being crude, rude whiners and complainers we can emulate our Father by blessing and releasing life through our conversations. We are warned not to allow anyone to deceive us with empty words. Empty words dull us into complacency—"It'll all be okay . . . It's not a big deal . . . Everyone else is doing it . . ." If words can be empty, then they can also be full. Words of life call us to better things. They remind us that we are not like everyone else because we are daughters of the Most High God. We are in the world, but not of it (John 17:15–16).

God, please reveal the difference between how the world operates and how You operate. I want to honor You with my words and actions, with not even a hint of anything else.

I Am Strong

BECAUSE I OPERATE BY GOD'S STANDARDS, NOT THE WORLD'S.

2

LEARNING OBEDIENCE

Blessed are all who fear the LORD, who walk in obedience to him.
PSALM 128:1

Often children exemplify, in a raw and obvious way, what adults have learned to gloss over. There was an incident when my second son, Austin, was little that captures how we can react when struggling to obey God.

When Austin was just two, some friends had come over to play. When it was time to leave, I decided to give each of the children gummy dinosaurs as a parting gift. I poured a generous amount of gummy dinosaurs into Austin's hand for him to pass out. As each child walked out the door they collected gummies, but when Austin got down to the last two he closed his fist tightly. There was one last girl waiting. I encouraged him, "Austin, there's lots more in the bag. Give her those two."

His only response was to run away and wrap himself around the mailbox post while shaking his head no. He was not going to budge.

I ran back into the house and offered the little girl gummies out of the bag. I waved goodbye to my friends and their children while trying to pry my son off the mailbox.

Once inside things got worse. The sweaty, smashed gummies were removed from my son's hand, and I sent Austin upstairs to his room until he calmed down.

"I'm not going to my room!" he declared, as he stomped out of the kitchen.

"Yes, you are," I countered calmly, remaining in the kitchen.

This exchange was repeated several times, but I noticed his voice was coming from farther and farther away. He was inching toward his room! After about fifteen minutes I heard him say emphatically, "I'm not going to sleep. I'm not going to take a nap!"

Then it was quiet. Later, I slipped upstairs and found him sound asleep on his bed.

At some level Austin knew he was wrong and even knew what he needed. That is why he put himself down for a nap. Why the exhausting protest? Why had he fought so hard?

Well, why do any of us fight obedience so hard? Besides being tired, I believe it is often for the same reason my son fought. He saw his pile of gummies dwindling and felt violated.

Honestly, I recognized myself in him. I've struggled with the same feelings of frustration that I don't know how to put into words. It is the very reason I've made silly declarations of independence as if to say, "God, I will obey but only under protest, and when I am ready."

As we mature, we learn not to pitch fits or react out of selfishness, but to trust that God knows what's best for us. It's so much less exhausting to do the right thing first than to get to it the hard way.

Lord, when I don't want to obey, teach me not to react
but to come to You first instead of last.

I Am Strong
WHEN I OBEY, WITHOUT STRUGGLING.

3

MADE HOLY

But just as he who called you is holy, so be holy in all you
do; for it is written: "Be holy, because I am holy."
1 PETER 1:15–16

God is holy . . . so we do holy. Holiness is not another failed attempt
of ours to try to be good; it is a revelation that we are His. Holiness
is more than a job description for ministers; it is a command for all who
assemble before the holy God. We are to be holy, for He is holy. We are
not asked to act holy or to appear holy; we are invited to *be* holy. To be
something means it becomes part of our essence or life force. We are filled
and led by His Spirit, which is holy—the Holy Spirit.

Holiness should influence our private interactions and our public
behavior. We can act holy but not be holy; we can look holy but not be
holy. To be something means it defines our very existence.

What does it mean to be holy? This Scripture lends us some insight:
"For he chose us in him before the creation of the world to be holy and
blameless in his sight" (Ephesians 1:4).

Before we drew our first breath, we were chosen. We were on His
mind before He created the earth. You were chosen by God in Christ and
destined to be holy and blameless. Because Jesus is both holy and blameless
we likewise inherit His standing before the Father.

Outside of Christ we were aliens to both His power and promises.

But on the cross, the curtain was rent in two. Everything that stood against us was nailed to the cross, and we were made one with God (Colossians 2:14).

To be holy is to be set apart—spirit, soul, and body. Simply put, holy means we are His.

Father, thank You for making me holy by Your supreme sacrifice. You are holy. Make everything I do bring me closer to You in holiness.

I Am Strong
BECAUSE I AM HOLY AND I AM HIS.

4

REFINED BY FIRE

---

*"See, I have refined you, though not as silver; I have
tested you in the furnace of affliction."*
ISAIAH 48:10

Gold and silver are refined in furnaces at such high temperatures that these metals liquefy. In this state, the dross and impurities rise to the surface and are apparent. The metallurgist skims off the dross before allowing the metal to cool and solidify. This process can be repeated until the metal is free of contaminants and alloys that weaken it.

God does not refine us in a literal furnace of fire. He has other ways to accomplish our refining process. He uses the furnace of affliction. A few synonyms for affliction are hardship, trouble, adversity, distress, and trial. Nobody likes affliction, but it's best to stay the course if we want to see the fruit of the process. This is important to remember, because when facing trials, it is not a matter of "if" but "when."

> When you pass through the waters, I will be with you; and when you pass through the rivers, they will not sweep over you. When you walk through the fire, you will not be burned; the flames will not set you ablaze. Isaiah 43:2

The afflictions of life can feel very much like floods and flames. None of us gets a pass that allows us to avoid these trials, but we are promised that they are just for a season. We pass through these hardships when we refuse to allow them to overwhelm us. Our Father knows what He is doing, and the refining process means that we will come out stronger on the other side.

Ultimately, God is more concerned with our condition than our comfort. This means He will allow life to become uncomfortable to expose our true condition. Very often this refining is set in motion by our prayers. Things will begin to heat up whenever we ask God to remove all that hinders our growth or displeases Him. Fiery trials are the means of revealing both our strengths and the errors of our ways. I challenge you to sing amidst the flames and allow your prayers of thanks to rise above the floodwaters, because God is refining you for His purpose and for your strength.

Dear Lord, open my eyes to recognize adversity and affliction for what they truly are, agents of my transformation. I know You will not abandon me in this refining process, so have Your way.

I Am Strong

WHEN I LET THE FIRES OF MY LIFE REFINE AND PURIFY MY HEART.

5

FASTING PHYSICALLY

Submit yourselves, then, to God. Resist the devil, and he will flee from you.
JAMES 4:7

Fasting is the ultimate in soul-weight reduction. A solely spiritual fast is when you abstain from a thought, action, or habit. A physical fast is the biblical practice of abstaining from food to seek God.

How is a physical fast different from a diet? One of the major differences is that a diet changes the way you look and a fast changes how you see. One shifts the scales, the other removes blinders (scales) from your eyes! Fasting expresses our submission to God. When we stop and drop to our knees in surrender to God, the enemy is overwhelmed with terror, and he runs! As we stop feeding on food, we are positioned to develop our hunger and thirst for the things of God. Our appetites are transformed as we feed on His Word and remember His goodness and love. Fasting brings with it a heightened awareness that also serves to tenderize our hearts.

If this is your first time fasting, start with something simple and healthy like fasting from unhealthy foods like white flour and sugar. You can read online about something called a Daniel fast. Or maybe your fast will mean skipping lunch. If you are going to do a water-only fast and have medical issues or are on medication, you should first consult a doctor.*

---

* This book is not intended to provide medical advice or to take the place of medical advice and treatment from your personal physician, so I advise you to consult your own doctor or other qualified health professionals regarding fasting if you have any concerns about it. If you are under age eighteen, do not fast without discussing it with your parents first.

Fasting is when you deny your flesh. It will be uncomfortable physically. But spiritually, this is a time of celebration, feasting, and joy! As you honor the King, He will honor you with His presence. Fasting is a sacred privilege, not a punishment.

Next, realize this is a life-and-death issue, because it is. You are putting bondage to death.

There is no sense in denying yourself food if you don't indulge yourself in God. Gather everything you need beforehand so you can just rest during your fast. Turn off your phone, computer (shut down your social media), and TV. Crank up the praise and worship music. This is a Sabbath time, so don't work on other things. Rest, sleep, and draw close to Him. Read the Word, including the book of Esther and the promises for fasting, or other Christian works that challenge you.

During the fast you are strengthening your spirit. Keep a journal of your prayer requests for this time. Be open and honest with your Father and record what He shows you through Scripture and prayer.

This a time to love, and I have every reason to believe He will give you living water and nourishment.

Lord God, as I fast, draw near to me. Shift my appetites and give me a hunger for more of You. I will quiet myself, believing You will speak. Increase my sensitivity and expose the things that have dulled me.

I Am Strong

BECAUSE AS I FAST, I AM FEASTING WITH MY KING.

6

OFFERING YOUR HEART

"Even now," declares the LORD, "return to me with all your heart, with fasting and weeping and mourning." Rend your heart and not your garments. Return to the LORD your God, for he is gracious and compassionate, slow to anger and abounding in love, and he relents from sending calamity.

JOEL 2:12–13

God's pursuit of us is relentless. No matter where we are, no matter what we've done, He will follow us to the ends of the earth. God cries out to this generation, "Even now when everything looks so hopeless, and you feel so dirty and helpless. Even now! When everyone else has failed, and everything you've tried has disappointed you . . . I will not. Even now! When it looks as though it is already too late . . . it's not! Return to Me with all your heart."

Because He pursues us, all we have to do is turn to Him. He invites us to be reasonable, to look bravely and truthfully at our condition, and realize it is not a pretty sight! Our sins are not a light shade of pink . . . they are screaming scarlet. But God doesn't want our crimson sacrifice, for the Prince has already paid the price. God longs to wash us clean. Instead of feeding us empty "food" that doesn't satisfy (the things we pursue in this world), He offers us the best of the land . . . if we are first willing, and then obedient. Willing to repent and say we've gone astray. Willing to serve Him with joy because He is good, faithful, and true. Willing to submit in obedience to His Word, for it is the law of love, life, and liberty. Willing to take up our cross and hide our life in Christ, the Word made flesh, and follow His example. The words of Joel call to us today: "Return to me with all your heart," no matter the state of your heart. The battle has always been for the hearts of women, and God is asking for your broken, bruised, and wounded one. He is inviting you to turn aside from the world's nightmares and step back into His dream, because from the beginning of time He's been searching for a bride . . . just like you.

Father, thank You for following me so closely that all I have to do is turn and fall into Your arms. I offer You my heart and return to You again.

I Am Strong
WHEN I TURN TOWARD THE ONE WHO PURSUES ME.

7

TAKING UP THE CROSS

Then he said to them all: "Whoever wants to be my disciple must deny themselves and take up their cross daily and follow me. For whoever wants to save their life will lose it, but whoever loses their life for me will save it."

LUKE 9:23–25

God has always longed for us to be His over our flawed human attempts to be good. He longs for us to see beyond the veil of religion and the works of the flesh and dare to draw near by faith, never doubting His goodness. He desires for us to worship Him in spirit and in truth, to take up our crosses daily and follow Him.

What does it mean when Jesus tells us to take up our cross? It is not as easy as attaching an ornament around our necks. It is to daily emblazon on our hearts that we are living sacrifices to Him. But our cross-carrying doesn't stop there; it extends to carrying the power and promise of what the cross purchased for each of us in a lost and dying world. The cross transforms everything.

In the Old Testament, the priests brought daily offerings before the Lord. "Solomon sacrificed burnt offerings to the LORD, according to the daily requirement for offerings commanded by Moses" (2 Chronicles 8:12–13). Taking up the cross is our daily offering. It is not a directive given by the laws of Moses, but from the Lord of life Himself.

Some may argue we don't need to carry a cross because Jesus was the final sacrifice, so it's a finished work. Our cross-carry is not a sin sacrifice. No offering we could possibly bring could satisfy the written statutes against us. Jesus alone did this by dying for our sins. His very life is hidden in God, as ours is to be hidden in His.

We don't have to shed our blood because He shed His. But being a living sacrifice means to live as He did, dead to sin, but alive to God! We offer ourselves—body and soul—to God as instruments of righteousness.

Mercy places us under grace, not the law, and in response to this gracious gift, we follow Christ's example of the cross. We daily yield to God and righteousness rather than to the flesh and wickedness. By an act of will, we lay our lives down and present our bodies. Then in faith we are drawn near to the heart of God, embracing the cross.

Jesus, thank You for going to the cross for me.
Teach me what it means to take up my cross, and
to live in obedience and thankfulness to You.

I Am Strong

WHEN I CARRY MY CROSS EACH DAY, OFFERING MYSELF AS A LIVING SACRIFICE.

8

THE WORD OF GOD

*Fix these words of mine in your hearts and minds; tie them as
symbols on your hands and bind them on your foreheads. . . .
Write them on the doorframes of your houses and on your gates,
so that your days and the days of your children may be many.*

DEUTERONOMY 11:18, 20–21

God exhorted the children of Israel to write His Word on the doorposts of their homes and hearts. Aside from meditating on or memorizing Scripture, I take this as an invitation to get creative! God's people certainly did. Hebrew men constructed small boxes called phylacteries, filled with tiny scrolls of Scripture, and they literally bound them on their foreheads, reminding them to obey the law. The Jewish mezuzah literally means "doorpost," and is a beautiful inscribed box hung over the door of a home, the scroll inside it bearing the words, "Hear, O Israel: The LORD our God, the LORD is one. Love the LORD your God with all your heart and with all your soul and with all your strength" (Deuteronomy 6:4–5). What a beautiful reminder! Why should we not do the same?

My sons have been known to tape the Scriptures they are meditating on to their mirrors. My husband listens to the Bible on CD in his car and to sermons at the gym. There are podcasts, worship music, and sermons online. It is actually really easy to incorporate God's Word in your daily life.

My grandchildren memorize verses to write them on their hearts. Some people get tattoos. If you do Scripture memorization as a family, post the passages several places and discuss how they can be practically applied. Or for private reflection consider journaling about how the verse could make a difference in your everyday life, in your relationships, and in your growth in the Lord.

Practical actions like these remind us that God's Word is present and applicable in every place, every situation, every intersection of our lives. Write, post, memorize, and repeat—until the words of God make it from your head to your heart.

Lord, show me creative ways to make Your Word an integral part of my everyday, practical life.

I Am Strong

WHEN I KEEP GOD'S WORDS ALWAYS BEFORE MY EYES AND ON MY MIND.

9

PERSEVERANCE

Consider it pure joy, my brothers and sisters, whenever you face trials of many
kinds, because you know that the testing of your faith produces perseverance.
JAMES 1:2–3

Really? Rough times are supposed to inspire joy? Once again you
see that our reaction of strength is counterintuitive to our culture's
response. After all, who would default to the response of "joy," let alone
of "pure joy," in the face of many kinds of trials? Yet this is exactly what
James, the brother of Jesus, is encouraging us to do. You see, it is in the
hard times rather than in the times of ease that we learn perseverance.
Some of the synonyms for this word are: purpose, drive, dedication,
resolve, grit, and determination. We will need all of these if we are to
stand strong in a world that seeks to compromise our strength. Another
definition referred to this quality of perseverance as "divine grace."

"Let perseverance finish its work so that you may be mature and
complete, not lacking anything" (James 1:4). In light of this promise of
completion and maturity, you can understand why James thought that
pure joy was an appropriate response. It is in the hard times of trial that
we discover where we have placed our trust or drawn our strength. It is in
the dry seasons of life that we discover the depth of our well. Seasons of
abundance rarely reveal what we are made of. In so many ways trials and
hardship are our spiritual strength trainers.

Let's look at the words of Paul to discover examples of trials in the time of the early apostles:

Three times I was beaten with rods, once I was pelted with stones, three times I was shipwrecked, I spent a night and a day in the open sea, I have been constantly on the move. I have been in danger from rivers, in danger from bandits, in danger from my fellow Jews, in danger from Gentiles; in danger in the city, in danger in the country, in danger at sea; and in danger from false believers. 2 Corinthians 11:25–26

And this list was just two of the verses Paul used to describe the challenges he had faced. When I read this list, I feel a bit weak in comparison. Today our list of challenges might read: unfollowed on social media, uninvited to a gathering of friends, unappreciated for what I do, unhappy with how I look or what I weigh. Perhaps in light of what the early church faced, it's time we all upped our strength level.

Heavenly Father, I choose to call trials pure joy, not because I enjoy them, but because I am thankful for the perseverance You will work in me through them.

I Am Strong

WHEN I KNOW WHAT TRIALS ARE WORKING IN ME.